Harvard
Business
Review

ON

COLLABORATING ACROSS SILOS

W9-BDR-423

THE HARVARD BUSINESS REVIEW PAPERBACK SERIES

The series is designed to bring today's managers and professionals the fundamental information they need to stay competitive in a fast-moving world. From the preeminent thinkers whose work has defined an entire field to the rising stars who will redefine the way we think about business, here are the leading minds and landmark ideas that have established the *Harvard Business Review* as required reading for ambitious businesspeople in organizations around the globe.

Other books in the series:

Other books in the series (continued):

Other books in the series (continued):

Harvard Business Review

ON

COLLABORATING

ACROSS SILOS

A HARVARD BUSINESS REVIEW PAPERBACK

Copyright 2009 Harvard Business School Publishing Corporation
All rights reserved
Printed in the United States of America
13 12 11 10 09   5 4 3 2 1

No part of this publication may be reproduced, stored in or introduced
into a retrieval system, or transmitted, in any form, or by any means
(electronic, mechanical, photocopying, recording, or otherwise),
without the prior permission of the publisher. Requests for permission
should be directed to permissions@hbsp.harvard.edu, or mailed to
Permissions, Harvard Business School Publishing, 60 Harvard Way,
Boston, Massachusetts 02163.

Library-of-Congress cataloging information available
ISBN 978-1-4221-7561-3

Contents

Eight Ways to Build Collaborative Teams

LYNDA GRATTON AND TAMARA J. ERICKSON

Executive Summary

EXECUTING COMPLEX INITIATIVES like acquisitions or an IT overhaul requires a breadth of knowledge that can be provided only by teams that are large, diverse, virtual, and composed of highly educated specialists. The irony is, those same characteristics have an alarming tendency to decrease collaboration on a team. What's a company to do?

Gratton, a London Business School professor, and Erickson, president of the Concours Institute, studied 55 large teams and identified those with strong collaboration despite their complexity. Examining the team dynamics and environment at firms ranging from Royal Bank of Scotland to Nokia to Marriott, the authors isolated eight success factors: (1) *"Signature" relationship*

1

practices that build bonds among the staff, in memorable ways that are particularly suited to a company's business. (2) *Role models of collaboration* among executives, which help cooperation trickle down to the staff. (3) *The establishment of a "gift culture,"* in which managers support employees by mentoring them daily, instead of a transactional "tit-for-tat culture." (4) *Training in relationship skills,* such as communication and conflict resolution. (5) *A sense of community,* which corporate HR can foster by sponsoring group activities. (6) *Ambidextrous leadership,* or leaders who are both task-oriented and relationship-oriented. (7) *Good use of heritage relationships,* by populating teams with members who know and trust one another. (8) *Role clarity and task ambiguity,* achieved by defining individual roles sharply but giving teams latitude on approach.

As teams have grown from a standard of 20 members to comprise 100 or more, team practices that once worked well no longer apply. The new complexity of teams requires companies to increase their capacity for collaboration, by making long-term investments that build relationships and trust, and smart near-term decisions about how teams are formed and run.

WHEN TACKLING A MAJOR INITIATIVE like an acquisition or an overhaul of IT systems, companies rely on large, diverse teams of highly educated specialists to get the job done. These teams often are convened quickly to meet an urgent need and work together virtually, collaborating online and sometimes over long distances.

Appointing such a team is frequently the only way to assemble the knowledge and breadth required to pull off many of the complex tasks businesses face today. When the BBC covers the World Cup or the Olympics, for instance, it gathers a large team of researchers, writers, producers, cameramen, and technicians, many of whom have not met before the project. These specialists work together under the high pressure of a "no retake" environment, with just one chance to record the action. Similarly, when the central IT team at Marriott sets out to develop sophisticated systems to enhance guest experiences, it has to collaborate closely with independent hotel owners, customer-experience experts, global brand managers, and regional heads, each with his or her own agenda and needs.

Our recent research into team behavior at 15 multinational companies, however, reveals an interesting paradox: Although teams that are large, virtual, diverse, and composed of highly educated specialists are increasingly crucial with challenging projects, those same four characteristics make it hard for teams to get anything done. To put it another way, the qualities required for success are the same qualities that undermine success. Members of complex teams are less likely—*absent other influences*—to share knowledge freely, to learn from one another, to shift workloads flexibly to break up unexpected bottlenecks, to help one another complete jobs and meet deadlines, and to share resources—in other words, to collaborate. They are less likely to say that they "sink or swim" together, want one another to succeed, or view their goals as compatible.

Consider the issue of size. Teams have grown considerably over the past ten years. New technologies help companies extend participation on a project to an ever greater number of people, allowing firms to tap into a wide body of knowledge and expertise. A decade or so ago, the common view was that true teams rarely had more than 20 members. Today, according to our research, many complex tasks involve teams of 100 or more. However, as the size of a team increases beyond 20 members, the tendency to collaborate naturally decreases, we have found. Under the right conditions, large teams can achieve high levels of cooperation, but creating those conditions requires thoughtful, and sometimes significant, investments in the capacity for collaboration across the organization.

Working together virtually has a similar impact on teams. The majority of those we studied had members spread among multiple locations—in several cases, in as many as 13 sites around the globe. But as teams became more virtual, we saw, cooperation also declined, unless the company had taken measures to establish a collaborative culture.

As for diversity, the challenging tasks facing businesses today almost always require the input and expertise of people with disparate views and backgrounds to create cross-fertilization that sparks insight and innovation. But diversity also creates problems. Our research shows that team members collaborate more easily and naturally if they perceive themselves as being alike. The differences that inhibit collaboration include not only nationality but also age, educational level, and even tenure. Greater diversity also often means that team members are working with people that they know only superficially or have never met before—colleagues drawn from other divisions of the company, perhaps, or even from outside it. We have found that the higher the proportion of strangers on the team and the greater the diversity of background and experience, the less likely the team members are to share knowledge or exhibit other collaborative behaviors.

In the same way, the higher the educational level of the team members is, the more challenging collaboration appears to be for them. We found that the greater the proportion of experts a team had, the more likely it was to disintegrate into nonproductive conflict or stalemate.

So how can executives strengthen an organization's ability to perform complex collaborative tasks—to maximize the effectiveness of large, diverse teams, while minimizing the disadvantages posed by their structure and composition?

To answer that question we looked carefully at 55 large teams and identified those that demonstrated high levels of collaborative behavior despite their complexity. Put differently, they succeeded both because of and despite their composition. Using a range of statistical analyses, we considered how more than 100 factors, such as the design of the task and the company culture, might contribute to collaboration, manifested, for example, in a willingness to share knowledge and workloads. Out of the 100-plus factors, we were able to isolate eight practices that correlated with success—that is, that appeared to help teams overcome substantially the difficulties that were posed by size, long-distance communication, diversity, and specialization. We then interviewed the teams that were very strong in these practices, to find out how they did it. In this article we'll walk through the practices. They fall into four general categories—executive support, HR practices, the strength of the team leader, and the structure of the team itself.

Executive Support

At the most basic level, a team's success or failure at collaborating reflects the philosophy of top executives in the organization. Teams do well when executives invest in supporting social relationships, demonstrate collaborative behavior themselves, and create what we call a "gift culture"—one in which employees experience interactions with leaders and colleagues as something valuable and generously offered, a gift.

INVESTING IN SIGNATURE RELATIONSHIP PRACTICES

When we looked at complex collaborative teams that were performing in a productive and innovative manner, we found that in every case the company's top executives had invested significantly in building and maintaining social relationships throughout the organization. However, the way they did that varied widely. The most collaborative companies had what we call "signature" practices—practices that were memorable, difficult for others to replicate, and particularly well suited to their own business environment.

For example, when Royal Bank of Scotland's CEO, Fred Goodwin, invested £350 million to open a new headquarters building outside Edinburgh in 2005, one of his goals was to foster productive collaboration among employees. Built around an indoor atrium, the new structure allows more than 3,000 people from the firm to rub shoulders daily.

The headquarters is designed to improve communication, increase the exchange of ideas, and create a sense of
community among employees. Many of the offices have
an open layout and look over the atrium—a vast transparent space. The campus is set up like a small town,
with retail shops, restaurants, jogging tracks and cycling
trails, spaces for picnics and barbecues—even a leisure
club complete with swimming pool, gym, dance studios,
tennis courts, and football pitches. The idea is that with
a private "Main Street" running through the headquarters, employees will remain on the campus throughout
the day—and be out of their offices mingling with colleagues for at least a portion of it.

To ensure that non-headquarters staff members feel
they are a part of the action, Goodwin also commis-
sioned an adjoining business school, where employees
from other locations meet and learn. The visitors are
encouraged to spend time on the headquarters campus
and at forums designed to give employees opportunities
to build relationships.

Indeed, the RBS teams we studied had very strong
social relationships, a solid basis for collaborative activity that allowed them to accomplish tasks quickly. Take
the Group Business Improvement (GBI) teams, which
work on 30-, 60-, or 90-day projects ranging from back-
office fixes to IT updates and are made up of people from
across RBS's many businesses, including insurance, retail
banking, and private banking in Europe and the United
States. When RBS bought NatWest and migrated the
new acquisition's technology platform to RBS's, the
speed and success of the GBI teams confounded many
market analysts.

BP has made another sort of signature investment.
Because its employees are located all over the world, with

relatively few at headquarters, the company aims to build social networks by moving employees across functions, businesses, and countries as part of their career development. When BP integrates an acquisition (it has grown by buying numerous smaller oil companies), the leadership development committee deliberately rotates employees from the acquired firm through positions across the corporation. Though the easier and cheaper call would be to leave the executives in their own units—where, after all, they know the business—BP instead trains them to take on new roles. As a consequence any senior team today is likely to be made up of people from multiple heritages. Changing roles frequently—it would not be uncommon for a senior leader at BP to have worked in four businesses and three geographic locations over the past decade—forces executives to become very good at meeting new people and building relationships with them.

MODELING COLLABORATIVE BEHAVIOR

In companies with many thousands of employees, relatively few have the opportunity to observe the behavior of the senior team on a day-to-day basis. Nonetheless, we found that the perceived behavior of senior executives plays a significant role in determining how cooperative teams are prepared to be.

Executives at Standard Chartered Bank are exceptionally good role models when it comes to cooperation, a strength that many attribute to the firm's global trading heritage. The Chartered Bank received its remit from Queen Victoria in 1853. The bank's traditional business was in cotton from Bombay (now Mumbai), indigo and tea from Calcutta, rice from Burma, sugar from Java, tobacco from Sumatra, hemp from Manila, and silk from Yokohama. The Standard Bank was founded in the Cape Province of South Africa in 1863 and was prominent in financing the development of the diamond fields and later gold mines. Standard Chartered was formed in 1969 through a merger of the two banks, and today the firm has 57 operating groups in 57 countries, with no home market.

It's widely accepted at Standard Chartered that members of the general management committee will frequently serve as substitutes for one another. The executives all know and understand the entire business and can fill in for each other easily on almost any task, whether it's leading a regional celebration, representing the company at a key external event, or kicking off an internal dialogue with employees.

While the behavior of the executive team is crucial to supporting a culture of collaboration, the challenge is to make executives' behavior visible. At Standard Chartered the senior team travels extensively; the norm is to travel even for relatively brief meetings. This investment in face-to-face interaction creates many opportunities for people across the company to see the top executives in action. Internal communication is frequent and open, and, maybe most telling, every site around the world is filled with photos of groups of executives—country and functional leaders—working together.

The senior team's collaborative nature trickles down throughout the organization. Employees quickly learn that the best way to get things done is through informal networks. For example, when a major program was recently launched to introduce a new customer-facing technology, the team responsible had an almost uncanny ability to understand who the key stakeholders at each branch bank were and how best to approach them. The team members' first-name acquaintance with people across the company brought a sense of dynamism to their interactions.

CREATING A "GIFT CULTURE"

A third important role for executives is to ensure that mentoring and coaching become embedded in their own routine behavior—and throughout the company. We looked at both formal mentoring processes, with clear roles and responsibilities, and less formal processes, where mentoring was integrated into everyday activities. It turned out that while both types were important, the latter was more likely to increase collaborative behavior. Daily coaching helps establish a cooperative "gift culture" in place of a more transactional "tit-for-tat culture."

At Nokia informal mentoring begins as soon as someone steps into a new job. Typically, within a few days, the employee's manager will sit down and list all the people in the organization, no matter in what location, it would be useful for the employee to meet. This is a deeply ingrained cultural norm, which probably originated when Nokia was a smaller and simpler organization. The manager sits with the newcomer, just as her manager sat with her when she joined, and reviews what topics the newcomer should discuss with each person on the list and why establishing a relationship with him or her is important. It is then standard for the newcomer to actively set up meetings with the people on the list, even when it means traveling to other locations. The gift of time—in the form of hours spent on coaching and building networks—is seen as crucial to the collaborative culture at Nokia.

Focused HR Practices

So what about human resources? Is collaboration solely in the hands of the executive team? In our study we looked at the impact of a wide variety of HR practices, including selection, performance management, promotion, rewards, and training, as well as formally sponsored coaching and mentoring programs.

We found some surprises: for example, that the type of reward system—whether based on team or individual achievement, or tied explicitly to collaborative behavior or not—had no discernible effect on complex teams' productivity and innovation. Although most formal HR programs appeared to have limited impact, we found that two practices did improve team performance: training in skills related to collaborative behavior, and support for informal community building. Where collaboration was strong, the HR team had typically made a significant investment in one or both of those practices—often in ways that uniquely represented the company's culture and business strategy.

ENSURING THE REQUISITE SKILLS

Many of the factors that support collaboration relate to what we call the "container" of collaboration—the underlying culture and habits of the company or team. However, we found that some teams had a collaborative culture but were not skilled in the practice of collaboration itself. They were encouraged to cooperate, they wanted to cooperate, but they didn't know how to work together very well in teams.

Our study showed that a number of skills were crucial: appreciating others, being able to engage in purposeful conversations, productively and creatively resolving conflicts, and program management. By training employees in those areas, a company's human resources or corporate learning department can make an important difference in team performance.

In the research, PricewaterhouseCoopers emerged as having one of the strongest capabilities in productive collaboration. With responsibility for developing 140,000 employees in nearly 150 countries, PwC's training includes modules that address teamwork, emotional intelligence, networking, holding difficult conversations, coaching, corporate social responsibility, and communicating the firm's strategy and shared values. PwC also teaches employees how to influence others effectively and build healthy partnerships.

A number of other successful teams in our sample came from organizations that had a commitment to teaching employees relationship skills. Lehman Brothers' flagship program for its client-facing staff, for instance, is its training in selling and relationship management. The program is not about sales techniques but, rather, focuses on how Lehman values its clients and makes sure that every client has access to all the resources the firm has to offer. It is essentially a course on strategies for building collaborative partnerships with customers, emphasizing the importance of trust-based personal relationships.

SUPPORTING A SENSE OF COMMUNITY

While a communal spirit can develop spontaneously, we discovered that HR can also play a critical role in cultivating it, by sponsoring group events and activities such as women's networks, cooking weekends, and tennis coaching, or creating policies and practices that encourage them.

At ABN Amro we studied effective change-management teams within the company's enterprise services function. These informal groups were responsible for projects associated with the implementation of new technology throughout the bank; one team, for instance, was charged with expanding online banking services. To succeed, the teams needed the involvement and expertise of different parts of the organization.

The ABN Amro teams rated the company's support for informal communities very positively. The firm makes the technology needed for long-distance collaboration readily available to groups of individuals with shared interests—for instance, in specific technologies or markets—who hold frequent web conferences and communicate actively online. The company also encourages employees that travel to a new location to arrange meetings with as many people as possible. As projects are completed, working groups disband but employees maintain networks of connections. These practices serve to build a strong community over time—one that sets the stage for success with future projects.

Committed investment in informal networks is also a central plank of the HR strategy at Marriott. Despite its size and global reach, Marriott remains a family business, and the chairman, Bill Marriott, makes a point of communicating that idea regularly to employees. He still tells stories of counting sticky nickels at night as a child—proceeds from the root-beer stand founded in downtown Washington, DC, by his mother and father.

Many of the firm's HR investments reinforce a friendly, family-like culture. Almost every communication reflects an element of staff appreciation. A range of "pop-up" events—spontaneous activities—create a sense of fun and community. For example, the cafeteria might roll back to the 1950s, hold a twist dance contest, and in doing so, recognize the anniversary of the company's first hotel opening. Bill Marriott's birthday might be celebrated with parties throughout the company, serving as an occasion to emphasize the firm's culture and values. The chairman recently began his own blog, which is popular with employees, in which he discusses everything from Marriott's efforts to become greener, to his favorite family vacation spots—themes intended to reinforce the idea that the company is a community.

The Right Team Leaders

In the groups that had high levels of collaborative behavior, the team leaders clearly made a significant difference. The question in our minds was how they actually achieved this. The answer, we saw, lay in their flexibility as managers.

ASSIGNING LEADERS WHO ARE BOTH TASK- AND RELATIONSHIP-ORIENTED

There has been much debate among both academics and senior managers about the most appropriate style for leading teams. Some people have suggested that relationship-oriented leadership is most appropriate in complex teams, since people are more likely to share knowledge in an environment of trust and goodwill. Others have argued that a task orientation—the ability to make objectives clear, to create a shared awareness of the dimensions of the task, and to provide monitoring and feedback—is most important.

In the 55 teams we studied, we found that the truth lay somewhere in between. The most productive, innovative teams were typically led by people who were *both* task- and relationship-oriented. What's more, these leaders changed their style during the project. Specifically, at the early stages they exhibited task-oriented leadership: They made the goal clear, engaged in debates about commitments, and clarified the responsibilities of individual team members. However, at a certain point in the development of the project they switched to a relationship orientation. This shift often took place once team members had nailed down the goals and their accountabilities and when the initial tensions around sharing knowledge had begun to emerge. An emphasis throughout a project on one style at the expense of the other inevitably hindered the long-term performance of the team, we found.

Producing ambidextrous team leaders—those with both relationship and task skills—is a core goal of team-leadership development at Marriott. The company's performance-review process emphasizes growth in both kinds of skills. As evidence of their relationship skills, managers are asked to describe their peer network and cite examples of specific ways that network helped them succeed. They also must provide examples of how they've used relationship building to get things done. The development plans that follow these conversations explicitly map out how the managers can improve specific elements of their social relationships and networks. Such a plan might include, for instance, having lunch regularly with people from a particular community of interest.

To improve their task leadership, many people in the teams at Marriott participated in project-management certification programs, taking refresher courses to maintain their skills over time. Evidence of both kinds of capabilities becomes a significant criterion on which people are selected for key leadership roles at the company.

Team Formation and Structure

The final set of lessons for developing and managing complex teams has to do with the makeup and structure of the teams themselves.

BUILDING ON HERITAGE RELATIONSHIPS

Given how important trust is to successful collaboration, forming teams that capitalize on preexisting, or "heritage," relationships, increases the chances of a project's success. Our research shows that new teams, particularly those with a high proportion of members who were strangers at the time of formation, find it more difficult to collaborate than those with established relationships.

Newly formed teams are forced to invest significant time and effort in building trusting relationships. However, when some team members already know and trust one another, they can become nodes, which over time evolve into networks. Looking closely at our data, we discovered that when 20% to 40% of the team members were already well connected to one another, the team had strong collaboration right from the start.

It helps, of course, if the company leadership has taken other measures to cultivate networks that cross boundaries. The orientation process at Nokia ensures that a large number of people on any team know one another, increasing the odds that even in a company of more than 100,000 people, someone on a companywide team knows someone else and can make introductions.

Nokia has also developed an organizational architecture designed to make good use of heritage relationships. When it needs to transfer skills across business functions or units, Nokia moves entire small teams intact instead of reshuffling individual people into new positions. If, for example, the company needs to bring together a group of market and technology experts to address a new customer need, the group formed would be composed of small pods of colleagues from each area. This ensures that key heritage relationships continue to strengthen over time, even as the organization redirects its resources to meet market needs. Because the entire company has one common platform for logistics, HR, finance, and other transactions, teams can switch in and out of businesses and geographies without learning new systems.

One important caveat about heritage relationships: If not skillfully managed, too many of them can actually disrupt collaboration. When a significant number of people within the team know one another, they tend to form strong subgroups—whether by function, geography, or anything else they have in common. When that happens, the probability of conflict among the subgroups, which we call fault lines, increases.

UNDERSTANDING ROLE CLARITY AND TASK AMBIGUITY

Which is more important to promoting collaboration: a clearly defined approach toward achieving the goal, or clearly specified roles for individual team members? The common assumption is that carefully spelling out the approach is essential, but leaving the roles of individuals within the team vague will encourage people to share ideas and contribute in multiple dimensions.

Our research shows that the opposite is true: Collaboration improves when the roles of individual team members are clearly defined and well understood—when individuals feel that they can do a significant portion of their work independently. Without such clarity, team members are likely to waste too much energy negotiating roles or protecting turf, rather than focus on the task. In addition, team members are more likely to want to collaborate if the path to achieving the team's goal is left somewhat ambiguous. If a team perceives the task as one that requires creativity, where the approach is not yet well known or predefined, its members are more likely to invest time and energy in collaboration.

At the BBC we studied the teams responsible for the radio and television broadcasts of the 2006 Proms (a two-month-long musical celebration), the team that televised the 2006 World Cup, and a team responsible for daytime television news. These teams were large— 133 people worked on the Proms, 66 on the World Cup, and 72 on the news—and included members with a wide range of skills and from many disciplines. One would imagine, therefore, that there was a strong possibility of confusion among team members.

To the contrary, we found that the BBC's teams scored among the highest in our sample with regard to the clarity with which members viewed their own roles and the roles of others. Every team was composed of specialists who had deep expertise in their given function, and each person had a clearly defined role. There was little overlap between the responsibilities of the sound technician and the camera operator, and so on. Yet the tasks the BBC teams tackle are, by their very nature, uncertain, particularly when they involve breaking news. The trick the BBC has pulled off has been to clarify team members' individual roles with so much precision that it keeps friction to a minimum.

The successful teams we studied at Reuters worked out of far-flung locations, and often the team members didn't speak a common language. (The primary languages were Russian, Chinese, Thai, and English.) These teams, largely composed of software programmers, were responsible for the rapid development of highly complex technical software and network products. Many of the programmers sat at their desks for 12 hours straight developing code, speaking with no one. Ironically, these teams judged cooperative behavior to be high among their members. That may be because each individual was given autonomy over one discrete piece of the project. The rapid pace and demanding project timelines encouraged individual members to work independently to get the job done, but each person's work had to be shaped with an eye toward the overall team goal.

Strengthening your organization's capacity for collaboration requires a combination of long-term investments—in building relationships and trust, in developing a culture in which senior leaders are role models of cooperation—and smart near-term decisions about the ways teams are formed, roles are defined, and challenges and tasks are articulated. Practices and structures that may have worked well with simple teams of people who were all in one location and knew one another are likely to lead to failure when teams grow more complex.

Most of the factors that impede collaboration today would have impeded collaboration at any time in history. Yesterday's teams, however, didn't require the same amount of members, diversity, long-distance cooperation, or expertise that teams now need to solve global business challenges. So the models for teams need to be realigned with the demands of the current business environment. Through careful attention to the factors we've described in this article, companies can assemble the breadth of expertise needed to solve complex business problems—without inducing the destructive behaviors that can accompany it.

The Research

OUR WORK is based on a major research initiative conducted jointly by the Concours Institute (a member of BSG Alliance) and the Cooperative Research Project of London Business School, with funding from the Advanced Institute for Management and 15 corporate sponsors. The initiative was created as a way to explore the practicalities of collaborative work in contemporary organizations.

We sent surveys to 2,420 people, including members of 55 teams. A total of 1,543 people replied, a response rate of 64%. Separate surveys were administered to group members, to group leaders, to the executives who evaluated teams, and to HR leaders at the companies involved. The tasks performed by the teams included new-product development, process reengineering, and identifying new solutions to business problems. The companies involved included four telecommunication companies, seven financial services or consulting firms, two media companies, a hospitality firm, and one oil company. The size of the teams ranged from four to 183 people, with an average of 44.

Our objective was to study the levers that executives could pull to improve team performance and innovation in collaborative tasks. We examined scores of possible factors, including the following:

The general culture of the company. We designed a wide range of survey questions to measure the extent to which the firm had a cooperative culture and to uncover employees' attitudes toward knowledge sharing.

Human resources practices and processes. We studied the way staffing took place and the process by which people were promoted. We examined the extent and type of training, how reward systems were configured, and the extent to which mentoring and coaching took place.

Socialization and network-building practices. We looked at how often people within the team participated in informal socialization, and the type of interaction that was most common. We also asked numerous questions about the extent to which team members were active in informal communities.

The design of the task. We asked team members and team leaders about the task itself. Our interest here was in how they perceived the purpose of the task, how complex it was, the extent to which the task required members of the team to be interdependent, and the extent to which the task required them to engage in boundary-spanning activities with people outside the team.

The leadership of the team. We studied the perceptions team members had of their leaders' style and how the leaders described their own style. In particular, we were interested in the extent to which the leaders practiced relationship-oriented and task-oriented skills and set cooperative or competitive goals.

The behavior of the senior executives. We asked team members and team leaders about their perceptions of the senior executives of their business unit. We focused in particular on whether team members described them as cooperative or competitive.

In total we considered more than 100 factors. Using a range of statistical analyses, we were able to identify eight that correlated with the successful performance of teams handling complex collaborative tasks. (See the insert "Eight Factors That Lead to Success.")

Collaboration Conundrums

FOUR TRAITS that are crucial to teams—but also undermine them

Large Size
Whereas a decade ago, teams rarely had more than 20 members, our findings show that their size has increased significantly, no doubt because of new technologies. Large teams are often formed to ensure the involvement of a wide stakeholder group, the coordination of a diverse set of activities, and the harnessing of multiple skills. As a consequence, many inevitably involve 100 people or more. However, our research shows that as the

size of the team increases beyond 20 members, the level of natural cooperation among members of the team decreases.

Virtual Participation

Today most complex collaborative teams have members who are working at a distance from one another. Again, the logic is that the assigned tasks require the insights and knowledge of people from many locations. Team members may be working in offices in the same city or strung across the world. Only 40% of the teams in our sample had members all in one place. Our research shows that as teams become more virtual, collaboration declines.

Diversity

Often the challenging tasks facing today's businesses require the rapid assembly of people from multiple backgrounds and perspectives, many of whom have rarely, if ever, met. Their diverse knowledge and views can spark insight and innovation. However, our research shows that the higher the proportion of people who don't know anyone else on the team and the greater the diversity, the less likely the team members are to share knowledge.

High Education Levels

Complex collaborative teams often generate huge value by drawing on a variety of deeply specialized skills and knowledge to devise new solutions. Again, however, our research shows that the greater the proportion of highly educated specialists on a team, the more likely the team is to disintegrate into unproductive conflicts.

Eight Factors That Lead to Success

1. **Investing in signature relationship practices.** Executives can encourage collaborative behavior by making highly visible investments—in facilities with open floor plans to foster communication, for example—that demonstrate their commitment to collaboration.

2. **Modeling collaborative behavior.** At companies where the senior executives demonstrate highly collaborative behavior themselves, teams collaborate well.

3. **Creating a "gift culture."** Mentoring and coaching—especially on an informal basis—help people build the networks they need to work across corporate boundaries.

4. **Ensuring the requisite skills.** Human resources departments that teach employees how to build relationships, communicate well, and resolve conflicts creatively can have a major impact on team collaboration.

5. **Supporting a strong sense of community.** When people feel a sense of community, they are more comfortable reaching out to others and more likely to share knowledge.

6. **Assigning team leaders that are both task- and relationship-oriented.** The debate has traditionally focused on whether a task or a relationship orientation creates better leadership, but in fact both are key to successfully leading a team. Typically, leaning more heavily on a task orientation at the outset

of a project and shifting toward a relationship orientation once the work is in full swing works best.

7. **Building on heritage relationships.** When too many team members are strangers, people may be reluctant to share knowledge. The best practice is to put at least a few people who know one another on the team.

8. **Understanding role clarity and task ambiguity.** Cooperation increases when the roles of individual team members are sharply defined yet the team is given latitude on how to achieve the task.

How Complex Is the Collaborative Task?

NOT ALL HIGHLY COLLABORATIVE tasks are complex. In assembling and managing a team, consider the project you need to assign and whether the following statements apply:

The task is unlikely to be accomplished successfully using only the skills within the team.

The task must be addressed by a new group formed specifically for this purpose.

The task requires collective input from highly specialized individuals.

The task requires collective input and agreement from more than 20 people.

The members of the team working on the task are in more than two locations.

The success of the task is highly dependent on understanding preferences or needs of individuals outside the group.

The outcome of the task will be influenced by events that are highly uncertain and difficult to predict.

The task must be completed under extreme time pressure.

If more than two of these statements are true, the task requires complex collaboration.

Originally published in November 2007
Reprint R0711F

Collaboration Rules

PHILIP EVANS AND BOB WOLF

Executive Summary

CORPORATE LEADERS SEEKING to boost growth, learning, and innovation may find the answer in a surprising place: the Linux open-source software community. Linux is developed by an essentially volunteer, self-organizing community of thousands of programmers. Most leaders would sell their grandmothers for workforces that collaborate as efficiently, frictionlessly, and creatively as the self-styled Linux hackers.

But Linux is software, and software is hardly a model for mainstream business. The authors have, nonetheless, found surprising parallels between the anarchistic, caffeinated, hirsute world of Linux hackers and the disciplined, tea-sipping, clean-cut world of Toyota engineering.

27

Specifically, Toyota and Linux operate by rules that blend the self-organizing advantages of markets with the low transaction costs of hierarchies. In place of markets' cash and contracts and hierarchies' authority are rules about how individuals and groups work together (with rigorous discipline); how they communicate (widely and with granularity); and how leaders guide them toward a common goal (through example).

Those rules, augmented by simple communication technologies and a lack of legal barriers to sharing information, create rich common knowledge, the ability to organize teams modularly, extraordinary motivation, and high levels of trust, which radically lowers transaction costs. Low transaction costs, in turn, make it profitable for organizations to perform more and smaller transactions—and so increase the pace and flexibility typical of high-performance organizations.

Once the system achieves critical mass, it feeds on itself. The larger the system, the more broadly shared the knowledge, language, and work style. The greater individuals' reputational capital, the louder the applause and the stronger the motivation. The success of Linux is evidence of the power of that virtuous circle. Toyota's success is evidence that it is also powerful in conventional companies.

CORPORATE LEADERS SEEKING growth, learning, and innovation may find the answer in a surprising place: the open-source software community. Unknowingly, perhaps, the folks who brought you Linux are virtuoso

practitioners of new work principles that produce
energized teams and lower costs. Nor are they alone.

By any measure, Linux is a powerfully competitive
product. It is estimated that more servers run on Linux
than on any other operating system. It has overwhelmed
UNIX as a commercial offering. And its advantages
extend beyond cost and quality to the speed with which
it is enhanced and improved. While partisans debate its
technical limitations and treatment of intellectual property, they agree that the product's success is inseparable
from its distinctive mode of production. Specifically,
Linux is the creation of an essentially voluntary, self-
organizing community of thousands of programmers
and companies. Most leaders would sell their grandmothers for workforces that collaborate as efficiently,
frictionlessly, and creatively as the self-styled Linux
"hackers."

But Linux is software, and software is kind of weird.
Toyota, however, is a company like any other—any other
consistently ranked among the world's top-performing
organizations, that is. The automaker has long been a
leader in quality and lean production, and the success
of the hybrid Prius has established its reputation as an
innovator. We have found that Toyota's managerial
methods resemble, in a number of their fundamentals,
the workings of the Linux community; the Toyota Production System (TPS) owes some of its vaunted respon-
siveness to open-source traits. In fact, Toyota itself is
evolving into a hybrid between a conventional hierarchy
and a Linux-like self-organizing network.

(Throughout this article, we use the term "Linux" as
shorthand for the free/open-source software community
that developed and continues to refine the operating
system and other open-source programs. We use

"Toyota" as shorthand for the Toyota Production System, which comprises Toyota and its direct—"tier one" in automotive parlance—suppliers in Japan and the United States.)

Toyota is remarkably similar to Linux in the way it blends key characteristics of both markets and hierarchies. Like markets, the Toyota and Linux communities can be self-organizing, but unlike markets, they don't use cash or contracts at critical junctures. Like hierarchies, Toyota and Linux enjoy low transaction costs, but unlike hierarchies, their members may belong to many different organizations (or to none at all) and are not corseted by specific, predefined roles and responsibilities. And like hierarchies, members share a common purpose, but that purpose emanates from self-motivation rather than from the external incentives or sanctions that hierarchies generally impose. In these respects, Toyota and Linux represent the best of both worlds. An analysis of their common characteristics suggests how high-performance organizations remain productive and inventive even under grueling conditions. We believe those lessons can significantly improve the way work in most organizations gets done.

Tuesday, December 2, 2003

Near midnight, Andrea Barisani, system administrator in the physics department of the University of Trieste, discovered that an attacker had struck his institution's Gentoo Linux server. He traced the breach to a vulnerable spot in the Linux kernel and another in rsync, a file transfer mechanism that automatically replicates data among computers. This was a serious attack: Any penetration of rsync could compromise files in thousands of servers worldwide.

Barisani woke some colleagues, who put him in touch with Mike Warfield, a senior researcher at Internet Security Systems in Atlanta, and with Andrew "Tridge" Tridgell, a well-known Linux programmer in Australia on whose doctoral thesis rsync was based. They directed Barisani's message (made anonymous for security reasons) to another Australian, Martin Pool, who worked for Hewlett-Packard in Canberra and had been a leader in rsync's development. Although Pool was no longer responsible for rsync (nobody was), he immediately hit the phones and e-mail, first quizzing Warfield and Dave Dykstra (another early contributor to rsync's development, who was based in California) about vulnerabilities and then helping Barisani trace the failure line by line.

By morning Trieste time, Pool and Barisani had found the precise location of the breach. Pool contacted the current rsync development group, while Barisani connected with the loose affiliation of amateurs and professionals that package Gentoo Linux, and he posted an early warning advisory to the Gentoo site. Pool and Paul "Rusty" Russell (a fellow Canberran who works for IBM) then labored through the Australian night to write a patch, and within five hours Gentoo user-developers started testing the first version. Meanwhile, Tridge crafted a description of the vulnerability and its fix, being sure (at Pool's urging) to credit Barisani and Warfield for their behind-the-scenes efforts. On Thursday afternoon Canberra time, the announcement and the patch were posted to the rsync Web site and thus distributed to Linux users worldwide.

A few days after the emergency, having caught up on his sleep, Barisani volunteered to collaborate with

Warfield in setting up a system of deliberately vulnerable servers to lure the system cracker into revealing himself.

No one authorized or directed this effort. No one— amateur or professional—was paid for participating or would have been sanctioned for not doing so. No one's job hinged on stopping the attack. No one clammed up for fear of legal liability. Indeed, the larger user community was kept informed of all developments. Yet despite the need for the highest security, a group of some 20 people, scarcely any of whom had ever met, employed by a dozen different companies, living in as many time zones and straying far from their job descriptions, accomplished in about 29 hours what might have taken colleagues in adjacent cubicles weeks or months.

It's tempting to dismiss this as an example of hacker weirdness—admirable, yes, but nothing to do with real business. Consider, however, another story.

Saturday, February 1, 1997

At 4:18 AM, a fire broke out in the Kariya Number 1 plant of Aisin Seiki, a major Japanese automotive parts supplier. Within minutes, the building and virtually all the specialized machinery inside were destroyed. Kariya Number 1 produces 99% of the brake fluid– proportioning valves, or P-valves, for Toyota's Japanese operations—parts required by every vehicle Toyota builds. And Toyota, true to its just-in-time principles, had less than a day's inventory. The Japanese Toyota Production System faced the possibility of a total shutdown lasting months.

Within hours, Aisin engineers met with their counterparts at Toyota and Toyota's other tier one suppliers. The group agreed to improvise as much production as possible. As news spread through the supplier network, some tier twos volunteered to play leadership roles. Aisin sent blueprints for the valves to any supplier that requested them and distributed whatever undamaged tools, raw materials, and work in process could be salvaged. Aisin and Toyota engineers helped jury-rig production lines in 62 locations—unused machine shops, Toyota's own prototyping shop, even a sewing machine facility owned by Brother. Denso, Toyota's largest supplier, volunteered to manage the messy logistics of shipping valves to Aisin for inspection and then on to Toyota's stalled assembly lines.

Everyone was surprised when a small tier two supplier of welding electrodes, Kyoritsu Sangyo, was first to deliver production-quality valves to Toyota—1,000 of them, just 85 hours after the fire. Others followed rapidly, and Toyota started reopening assembly lines on Wednesday. Roughly two weeks after the halt, the entire supply chain was back to full production. Six months later, Aisin distributed an emergency response guide containing lessons drawn from the experience and recommending procedures for responding to such situations in the future.

No one individual or organization planned this effort: rather, people and companies stepped in where they could. Competitors collaborated. No one at the time was paid for contributing. Months later, Aisin compensated the other companies for the direct costs of the valves they had delivered. Toyota gave each tier one supplier an honorarium based on current sales to the automaker, encouraging—but not requiring—them to do likewise for their own tier twos.

Few communities appear more different than the anarchistic, caffeinated, hirsute world of hackers and the disciplined, tea-sipping, clean-cut world of Japanese auto engineering. But the parallels between these stories are striking. In both of them, individuals found one another and stepped into roles without a plan or an established command-and-control structure. An extended human network organized itself in hours and "swarmed" against a threat. People, teams, and companies worked together without legal contracts or negotiated payment. And despite the lack of any authoritarian stick or financial carrot, those people worked *like hell* to solve the problem.

Now, obviously, these were emergency responses. But a look at the day-to-day operations of the Linux community and the Toyota Production System reveals that those responses were merely intensifications of the way people were already working.

Obsession, Interaction, and a Light Touch

The rules of markets are about cash and contracts. The rules of hierarchies are about authority and accountability. But at the core of the Linux and Toyota communities are rules about three entirely different things: how individuals and small groups work together; how, and how widely, they communicate; and how leaders guide them toward a common goal.

A COMMON WORK DISCIPLINE

The Linux and Toyota communities are both composed of engineers, so members have the same skills as their colleagues and speak the same language. But these groups are far more disciplined and rigorous in their approach to work than are other engineering communities. Both emphasize granularity: They pay attention to small details, eliminate problems at the source, and trim anything resembling excess, whether it be work, code, or material. Linux members, for example, share an obsession with writing minimal code, compiling each day's output before proceeding to the next and extirpating programming flaws as they go along. For their part, TPS engineers are relentless in applying short cycles of trial and error, focusing on just one thing at a time, and getting inside and observing actual processes. Both groups carry those principles to apparent extremes. Linux programmers whittle away at code in pursuit not of computational efficiency but of elegance. Toyota engineers reject stampings for the Lexus hood—while flawless and entirely within spec—because the sheen, to their eyes, lacks luster.

WIDESPREAD, GRANULAR COMMUNICATION

In both the Linux and Toyota communities, information about problems and solutions is shared widely, frequently, and in small increments. Most Linux hacker communication is not between individuals but by postings to open, searchable Listservs. Anyone can review the version history of the code and the Listserv debates—not executive summaries or abstracts but the raw activity itself. And every code contribution is stress tested by scores of people. As a famous open-source mixed metaphor puts it: "With a thousand eyes, all bugs are shallow." The median upload to the Linux kernel is a mere dozen lines of code. The working alpha version is recompiled every 24 hours, so hackers reconcile their efforts almost continuously. If someone worked in isolation for six months on even the most brilliant contribution, it would probably be rejected for lack of compatibility with the others' efforts.

The Toyota philosophy of continuous improvement likewise comprises a thousand small collaborations. Toyota engineers are famously drilled to "ask why five times" to follow a chain of causes and effects back to a problem's root. This is not a vapid cliché about thinking deeply. Quite the contrary, in fact. The precept's merit is precisely in its superficiality. Saying that B causes A is simplistic—all the complexities of multiple interactions boiled down to a single cause and effect. But the chain of thought required to discover that C causes B, and D causes C, quickly takes you into a new domain, probably someone else's. So rather than concoct complex solutions within their own domains, engineers must seek simple ones beyond them. "Doing your why-whys," as the practice is known, is not about depth at all—it's about breadth.

And as with Linux, Toyota's communication protocols enforce this discipline. Each meeting addresses just one topic and drives toward a specific outcome, even if that means the same people meet more than once in a day. Lessons are written in a standard format on a single sheet of A3 paper. And everyone learns how to craft these reports, down to the fold in the document that shows the main points and conceals the details.

LEADERS AS CONNECTORS

At every level, Linux and TPS leaders play three critical roles. They instruct community members—often by example—in the disciplines we've just described. They articulate clear and simple goals for each project based on their strategic vision. And they connect people, by

merit of being very well connected themselves. The top
Linux programmers process upwards of 300 or 400
e-mails daily. Fujio Cho, the president of Toyota, manages by similarly numerous daily interactions that transcend the normal chain of command.

Neither community treats leading as a discipline distinct from doing. Rather, the credibility and, therefore,
authority of leaders derives from their proficiency as
practitioners. The content of leaders' staccato communi-
cations is less *about* work than it *is* work. (When Linux
creator Linus Torvalds dashes off his scores of daily
e-mails, he writes almost as much in the C programming
language as he does in English.)

Occasionally, leaders do have to perform traditional
leadership acts, such as arbitrating conflicts. That, however, is the exception and is viewed as a bit of a system
failure. The default assumption is that, as far as possible,
managers don't manage in a traditional sense: The
human network manages itself. In Linux, development
priorities are decided not by a CEO but by thousands of
hackers voting with their feet by choosing what to work
on. That kind of radical self-management does not happen at Toyota, except in emergencies. But even in daily
operations, a single production worker who sees a quality problem can stop the line, and project teams have
wide latitude to tap resources, make purchase decisions,
and pursue priorities they set for themselves.

Taken together, these three principles seed a continuously adapting system. Over and over, ideas are formulated in tight, testable packets; they are communicated
with minimal attenuation through established, direct,
person-to-person connections; and where links are
absent, widely connected leader-practitioners create
them as needed. This is discipline, but not the discipline

of conformity produced by controls and incentives. Rather, it resembles the discipline of science. Like scientific communities, these systems rely on common procedures, common rules for communication and testing, and common goals clearly understood. Individual behavior is rigorously cautious, but collective achievement is marked by continuous, radical innovation.

What They Know and How They Know It

At the heart of Linux and the Toyota Production System, then, is a set of work, communication, and leadership practices that contributes to a new form of collaboration. This collaboration also relies on two infrastructure components: a shared pool of knowledge and universally available tools for moving knowledge around.

COMMON INTELLECTUAL PROPERTY

The General Public License under which Linux is published requires that all distributors make their source code freely available so that others can freely emend it. This viral principle prevents code from being stowed away in proprietary products. That transparency, in turn, breaks down the distinction between producer and user. A sophisticated "customer" like Andrea Barisani is really a user-developer, who fixes flaws and adds features for his own benefit, then shares those improvements with everyone else. Such a role is impossible when proprietary code is licensed from a commercial vendor. Similarly, Toyota's supply chain is predicated on the principle that while product knowledge (such as a blueprint) is someone's intellectual property, process knowledge is shared. That breaks down some distinctions among companies.

Toyota's suppliers regularly share extensive process improvement lessons both vertically and laterally, even with their competitors. In Japan, suppliers are generally exclusive to a single OEM, so the collective benefit of that shared information stays within the Toyota supply chain. But even in the United States, where Toyota is just one of several customers for most of its tier ones, the carmaker does the same thing through its Bluegrass Automotive Manufacturers Association, which disseminates best practices to all members.

SIMPLE, PERVASIVE TECHNOLOGY

Although information is the lifeblood of the Linux and TPS communities, their circulation systems are surprisingly rudimentary. Linux developers produce state-of-the-art software using communication technology no more sophisticated than e-mail and Listservs— but those mundane tools are used by everyone.

Indeed, so great is the value placed on universality that plain-text, rather than formatted, e-mails are the norm, ensuring that messages will appear exactly the same to all recipients. Toyota, whose products are state-of-the-art as well, also prefers simple and pervasive internal technology. An empty kanban bin signals the need for parts replenishment; a length of duct tape on the assembly-line floor allots the completion times of tasks on a moving vehicle. Quality control problems on the assembly line are announced via pagers and TV monitors. And everyone gets the alert. Even Ray Tanguay, head of Toyota Canada, is paged whenever a flaw is found in the latest Lexus consignment on the dock in Long Beach, California, or in a service bay anywhere in North America.

The Power of Trust and Applause

Such extremely rich, flexible collaborations have positive psychological consequences for participants and powerful competitive ones for their organizations. Those consequences are rich common knowledge, the ability to organize teams modularly, extraordinary motivation, and high levels of trust.

RICH SEMANTIC KNOWLEDGE

A rigorous work discipline, common intellectual property, and constant sharing combine to distribute knowledge widely and relatively evenly across human networks. That knowledge includes not just the formal, syntactic information found in databases but also the semantically rich, ambiguous knowledge about content and process that is the currency of creative collaboration. What do we mean by the sheen of a body stamping having insufficient luster? What, precisely, must we discuss with the steel company to correct such an ill-defined problem? This kind of no-easy-answer question is continually discussed and resolved in a thousand small-team collaborations. The resulting nuanced thinking and richer common vocabulary on such matters are fed back into the knowledge pool, where they are available for further refinement by the whole community.

MODULAR TEAMING

Modularity is a design principle by which a complex process or product is divided into simple parts connected by standard rules. In modular arrangements of teams, each team focuses on small, simple tasks that together make up a larger whole. Modularity allows an organization to run multiple, parallel experiments, making many small bets instead of a few large ones. The Toyota suppliers organized themselves this way to make P-valves, operating partly by direction but chiefly by volunteering to do what each knew best. The Gentoo group, Tridge's security experts, and Pool's circle of rsync alumni were preexisting and overlapping modules that mixed and matched roles as the emergency required.

When we mapped the patterns of day-to-day collaboration across the entire Linux kernel development effort, we found that such modular arrangements are pervasive and, to a degree, nest within one another. This creates a kind of dynamic organization chart—a chart that nobody wrote but one that enables the community to expand and adapt without collapsing into chaos.

INTRINSIC MOTIVATION

The Linux and TPS communities dissociate money from key transactions. Yet despite weak financial incentives, they command a level of motivation higher than that found in conventional environments. Monetary carrots and accountability sticks, psychologists have consistently found, motivate people to perform narrow, specified tasks but generally discourage people from going beyond them. Admiration and applause are far more effective stimulants of above-and-beyond behavior. "The personal reputation of the developer is attached to every release," Linus Torvalds explained to technology columnist Robert Cringely in 1998. "If you are making something to give away to the world, something that represents to millions of users your philosophy of computing, you will always make it the very best product you can."

Psychologists also emphasize the motivational importance of autonomy. Linux programmers decide for themselves how and where to contribute, and they enjoy the satisfaction of producing something whose quality is defined not by a marketing department nor by accountants but by their own exacting standards. Coauthor Bob Wolf and MIT's Karim Lakhani surveyed more than 800 user-developers, and over half said that their open-source work is the most valuable and creative endeavor in their professional lives.

The Toyota Production System doesn't offer such extreme autonomy, of course, and employees don't work for free. But compared with their counterparts in the rest of the auto industry, TPS workers enjoy fewer controls, greater encouragement of individual initiative, fewer metrics attached to individual performance, and louder peer applause. Professional and corporate pride, not Toyota's honorarium, was the payoff for the team at Kyoritsu Sangyo when it delivered the first batch of P-valves. That same pride is felt by a junior assembly-line worker when he is trusted by his peers to experiment with process improvements and to stop the line if something goes wrong.

HIGH LEVELS OF TRUST

When information flows freely, reputation, more than reciprocity, becomes the basis for trust. Operating under constant scrutiny—which is challenging but not hostile—workers know their reputations are at risk, and that serves as a guarantor of good behavior, the equivalent of

contracts in a market or audits in a hierarchy. Hence the
obsession in the Linux community with acknowledging
code contributions and including personal e-mail
addresses in the comment fields of Listservs. Hence the
generous public credit bestowed on Barisani and
Warfield. Hence the collective celebration of Kyoritsu
Sangyo's heroic efforts.

With their reputations at stake, people are less likely
to act opportunistically. With the same information
available to everyone, there is less chance that one party
will exploit another's ignorance. And with a common
vocabulary and way of working, fewer misunderstand-
ings occur. Those factors drive up trust, the fundamental
social capital of these communities.

Trust would matter less if there were no cost to exit-
ing these networks or if transactions were of radically
different sizes (since that would tempt people or companies to break the rules when a big opportunity arose).
But in both the Linux and Toyota communities, entry
to the inner circle is a hard-earned privilege, and both
operate on many small exchanges.

And, of course, where trust is the currency, reputation is a source of power. In a sparse network, such
as most markets and hierarchies, power derives from
controlling or brokering the flow of information and
often, therefore, from restricting it. In a dense network,
however, information simply flows around the would-be
choke point. Under those circumstances, there is more
power in being an information source than an information sink. Consequently, individuals are motivated to
maximize both the visibility of their work and their
connections to those who are themselves broadly connected. That, in turn, feeds the information density
of the network.

Cheap Transactions and Plenty of Them

So far we have been discussing the content of work.
But the TPS and Linux models change the economics
of work as well, by driving down transaction costs.
Low transaction costs make it profitable for organizations to perform more and smaller transactions—
both internal and external—and so increase the
pace and flexibility typical of high-performance
organizations.

The classical sources of transaction costs are
mutual vulnerability in the face of uncertainty,
conflicting interests, and unequal access to information. We spend cash on negotiation, supervision, and
restitution to reduce those imperfections. Both
markets and hierarchies incur transaction costs
(though hierarchies exist to economize on them, as
Ronald Coase and Oliver Williamson have argued).
Using a methodology developed by J.J. Wallis and
Douglass North, we estimate that in the year 2000, cash
transaction costs alone accounted for over half the
nongovernmental U.S. GDP! We spend more money
negotiating and enforcing transactions than we do
fulfilling them.

In the Linux and Toyota communities, agreements
are enforced not by the sanction of a legal contract, nor
by the authority of a boss, but by mutual trust—lowering
transaction costs dramatically. This is not new: Teams
of people everywhere in the conventional work-place
operate on the basis of trust.

What is new is how widely trust can extend, even to
people who don't know each other—or even among
those who have competing interests. Aisin trusted its
rival suppliers with the P-valve blueprints. The rsync

hackers swapped sensitive information with people they had never met. Toyota's component suppliers share process knowledge daily, trusting that Toyota will not use it to beat down prices. Linux hackers trust one another to make uncoordinated and simultaneous emendations in the code base.

Moreover, holding property in common—as certain kinds of intellectual property are held within these communities—lowers the monetary stakes among the joint owners. Transaction costs fall because there is simply less to negotiate over. In the Linux community, transaction costs approach zero. Hewlett-Packard paid Martin Pool to be a Linux engineer, but it does not follow that HP needed to be paid on the margin for Pool's nocturnal labors on rsync. In the Toyota community, transaction costs, while not zero, have been radically reduced. When the Aisin Seiki plant was destroyed, Toyota and its suppliers didn't sue one another or cobble together emergency supply contracts. They simply got on with the job, trusting that fair restitution would eventually be made. Jeffrey Dyer, a professor of strategy at Brigham Young University, estimates that transaction costs between Toyota and its tier one suppliers are just one-eighth those at General Motors, a disparity he attributes to different levels of trust.

A Model for Many

Bring together all these elements and you have a virtuous circle. A dense, self-organizing network creates the conditions for large-scale trust. Large-scale trust drives down transaction costs. Low transaction costs, in turn, enable lots of small transactions, which create a cumulatively deepening, self-organized network.

Once the system achieves critical mass, it feeds on itself. The larger the system, the more broadly shared the knowledge, language, and work style. The greater individuals' reputational capital, the louder the applause and the stronger the motivation. The success of Linux is evidence of the power of that virtuous circle. Toyota's success is evidence that it is also powerful in conventional, profit-maximizing companies.

The Linux community and Toyota Production System are strikingly different. The fact that they achieve so much in such similar ways points to some principles others can follow.

- The discipline of science is surprisingly adaptable to the organization of corporate—and even intercorporate—work.

- Under some circumstances, trust is a viable substitute for market contracts and hierarchical authority, not just in small teams but also in very large communities.

- Across supply chains, organizations that are able to substitute trust for contracts gain more from the collaboration than they lose in bargaining power.

- Low transaction costs buy more innovation than do high monetary incentives.

These principles serve businesses' need for growth and innovation in ways that traditional organizational models do not. And perhaps the effectiveness of these collaborations suggests the ultimate emergence of something altogether new. Not markets. Not hierarchies. But a powerful combination of both—and a signature of the networked society.

Building Vibrant Human Networks

COMPANIES LAYING THE groundwork for high-performance collaboration should follow these principles:

Deploy pervasive collaborative technology. Keep it simple and open: "small pieces loosely joined," in *Cluetrain Manifesto* coauthor David Weinberger's felicitous phrase. Tools should work together through common standards and be as compatible as possible with those of the rest of the world. Think options not integration, adaptability not static efficiency.

Keep work visible. Unless there is a really good reason not to, let everybody see everybody's real work. Let people learn to filter and sort for themselves. Don't abstract, summarize, or channel. Fodder is good. Put it within everyone's reach.

Build communities of trust. When people trust one another, they are more likely to collaborate freely and productively. When people trust their organizations, they are more likely to give of themselves now in anticipation of future reward. And when organizations trust each other, they are more likely to share intellectual property without choking on legalisms.

Think modularly. Reengineering was about thinking linearly: managing the end-to-end process instead of discrete functions. That approach fosters focused efficiency but inhibits variety and adaptability. Modularity is the reverse: sacrificing static efficiency for the recombinant value of options.

Think modular teams as well as processes. The finer, the better.

Encourage teaming. Celebrate the sacrifices that teams make for the broader enterprise, including customers and suppliers. Dismantle individualized performance metrics and rewards that pit people against one another. Cheap transactions among the many fuel more innovation than expensive incentives aimed at the few. Reward the group, and the group will reward you.

Exploiting the Neglected 80%

THE PARETO PRINCIPLE famously dictates that companies derive 80% of their value from just 20% of their products, customers, or ideas. Because of high transaction costs, the long tail of that curve— that 80% of uncertain value generators—cannot be explored. So in the name of company focus, the tail gets lopped off, segmented away, or reengineered out of existence. Potentially profitable innovations die with it.

Organizations that reduce transaction costs can embrace the rejected 80%. They can respond to weak market signals, tap small segments, and experiment with unlikely combinations of technologies. They can place a hundred small bets instead of a few big ones.

For example, Detroit considered hybrid vehicles to be an uninteresting intermediate product: U.S. auto executives preferred so-far-unfulfilled research on fuel cell technology. Meanwhile, Toyota was building the Prius. The hybrid is now in its second generation, and Toyota expects to sell 300,000 worldwide this year. Toyota's low transaction costs and penchant for small-scale collaborations helped it keep open 80 discrete options for the hybrid engine until just six months before delivering a final design. Conventional automakers would have needed to freeze those design variables at least two years earlier.

It is in the interstices of the human network— rather than in the minds of a few wunderkinder— that most real innovations are born. And so it is transaction costs that constrain innovation by constraining opportunities to share different and conflicting ideas, skills, and prejudices.

"Detroit people are far more talented than people at Toyota," remarks Toyota president Fujio Cho, with excessive modesty. "But we take averagely talented people and make them work as spectacular teams." The network, in other words, is the innovator.

Giving Credit Where Credit Is Due

THE LINUX COMMUNITY uses a particular format—a "credit file"—to acknowledge the contributions of its members. If we, for instance, were to acknowledge in the Linux format the contributions of individuals who helped shape our thinking for this article, here's how it would look:

n: Mark Blaxill

e: blaxill.mark@bcg.com

d: Exploration of economics of open source

s: Boston Consulting Group

n: Paul Carlile

e: carlile@bu.edu

d: Discussion of Linux/Toyota parallels

s: Boston University

n: Karim Lakhani

e: lakhani@mit.edu

d: Discussion of Linux/Toyota parallels

d: Survey of free/open source hackers

s: MIT

Originally published in July 2005
Reprint R0507H

Want Collaboration?

*Accept—and Actively
Manage—Conflict*

JEFF WEISS AND JONATHAN HUGHES

Executive Summary

COMPANIES TRY ALL KINDS of ways to improve
collaboration among different parts of the organization: cross-unit incentive systems, organizational
restructuring, team-work training. While these initiatives produce occasional success stories, most have
only limited impact in dismantling organizational
silos and fostering collaboration.

The problem? Most companies focus on the
symptoms ("Sales and delivery do not work
together as closely as they should") rather than on
the root cause of failures in cooperation: conflict.
The fact is, you can't improve collaboration until
you've addressed the issue of conflict. The authors
offer six strategies for effectively managing conflict:

• Devise and implement a common method for
resolving conflict.

- Provide people with criteria for making trade-offs.
- Use the escalation of conflict as an opportunity for coaching.
- Establish and enforce a requirement of joint escalation.
- Ensure that managers resolve escalated conflicts directly with their counterparts.
- Make the process for escalated conflict-resolution transparent.

The first three strategies focus on the point of conflict; the second three focus on escalation of conflict up the management chain. Together they constitute a framework for effectively managing discord, one that integrates conflict resolution into day-to-day decision-making processes, thereby removing a barrier to cross-organizational collaboration.

THE CHALLENGE IS A long-standing one for senior managers: How do you get people in your organization to work together across internal boundaries? But the question has taken on urgency in today's global and fast-changing business environment. To service multinational accounts, you increasingly need seamless collaboration across geographic boundaries. To improve customer satisfaction, you increasingly need collaboration among functions ranging from R&D to distribution. To offer solutions tailored to customers' needs, you increasingly need collaboration between product and service groups.

Meanwhile, as competitive pressures continually force companies to find ways to do more with less, few managers have the luxury of relying on their own dedicated staffs to accomplish their objectives. Instead, most must work with and through people across the organization, many of whom have different priorities, incentives, and ways of doing things.

Getting collaboration right promises tremendous benefits: a unified face to customers, faster internal decision making, reduced costs through shared resources, and the development of more innovative products. But despite the billions of dollars spent on initiatives to improve collaboration, few companies are happy with the results. Time and again we have seen management teams employ the same few strategies to boost internal cooperation. They restructure their organizations and reengineer their business processes. They create cross-unit incentives. They offer teamwork training. While such initiatives yield the occasional success story, most of them have only limited impact in dismantling organizational silos and fostering collaboration—and many are total failures. (See the insert "The Three Myths of Collaboration" at the end of the article.)

So what's the problem? Most companies respond to the challenge of improving collaboration in entirely the wrong way. They focus on the symptoms ("Sales and delivery do not work together as closely as they should") rather than on the root cause of failures in cooperation: conflict. The fact is, you can't improve collaboration until you've addressed the issue of conflict.

This can come as a surprise to even the most experienced executives, who generally don't fully appreciate

the inevitability of conflict in complex organizations.
And even if they do recognize this, many mistakenly
assume that efforts to increase collaboration will significantly reduce that conflict, when in fact some of these
efforts—for example, restructuring initiatives—actually
produce more of it.

Executives underestimate not only the inevitability of
conflict but also—and this is key—its importance to the
organization. The disagreements sparked by differences
in perspective, competencies, access to information, and
strategic focus within a company actually generate much
of the value that can come from collaboration across
organizational boundaries. Clashes between parties are
the crucibles in which creative solutions are developed
and wise trade-offs among competing objectives are
made. So instead of trying simply to reduce disagreements, senior executives need to embrace conflict and,
just as important, institutionalize mechanisms for
managing it.

Even though most people lack an innate understanding of how to deal with conflict effectively, there
are a number of straightforward ways that executives
can help their people—and their organizations—
constructively manage it. These can be divided into
two main areas: strategies for managing disagreements
at the point of conflict and strategies for managing
conflict upon escalation up the management chain.
These methods can help a company move through
the conflict that is a necessary precursor to truly
effective collaboration and, more important, extract
the value that often lies latent in intra-organizational
differences. When companies are able to do both,
conflict is transformed from a major liability into
a significant asset.

Strategies for Managing Disagreements at the Point of Conflict

Conflict management works best when the parties involved in a disagreement are equipped to manage it themselves. The aim is to get people to resolve issues on their own through a process that improves—or at least does not damage—their relationships. The following strategies help produce decisions that are better informed and more likely to be implemented.

DEVISE AND IMPLEMENT A COMMON METHOD FOR RESOLVING CONFLICT

Consider for a moment the hypothetical Matrix Corporation, a composite of many organizations we've worked with whose challenges will likely be familiar to managers. Over the past few years, salespeople from nearly a dozen of Matrix's product and service groups have been called on to design and sell integrated solutions to their customers. For any given sale, five or more lead salespeople and their teams have to agree on issues of resource allocation, solution design, pricing, and sales strategy. Not surprisingly, the teams are finding this difficult. Who should contribute the most resources to a particular customer's offering? Who should reduce the scope of their participation or discount their pricing to meet a customer's budget? Who should defer when disagreements arise about account strategy? Who should manage key relationships within the customer account? Indeed, given these thorny questions, Matrix is finding that a single large sale typically generates far more conflict inside the company than it does with the customer. The resulting wasted time and damaged relationships

among sales teams are making it increasingly difficult
to close sales.

Most companies face similar sorts of problems. And,
like Matrix, they leave employees to find their own ways
of resolving them. But without a structured method for
dealing with these issues, people get bogged down not
only in what the right result should be but also in how to
arrive at it. Often, they will avoid or work around conflict, thereby forgoing important opportunities to collaborate. And when people do decide to confront their
differences, they usually default to the approach they
know best: debating about who's right and who's wrong
or haggling over small concessions. Among the negative
consequences of such approaches are suboptimal, "split-
the-difference" resolutions—if not outright deadlock.

Establishing a companywide process for resolving disagreements can alter this familiar scenario. At the very
least, a well-defined, well-designed conflict resolution
method will reduce transaction costs, such as wasted
time and the accumulation of ill will, that often come
with the struggle to work though differences. At best, it
will yield the innovative outcomes that are likely to
emerge from discussions that draw on a multitude of
objectives and perspectives. There is an array of conflict
resolution methods a company can use. But to be effective, they should offer a clear, step-by-step process for
parties to follow. They should also be made an integral
part of existing business activities—account planning,
sourcing, R&D budgeting, and the like. If conflict resolution is set up as a separate, exception-based process—a
kind of organizational appeals court—it will likely wither
away once initial managerial enthusiasm wanes.

At Intel, new employees learn a common method and
language for decision making and conflict resolution.

The company puts them through training in which they learn to use a variety of tools for handling discord. Not only does the training show that top management sees disagreements as an inevitable aspect of doing business, it also provides a common framework that expedites conflict resolution. Little time is wasted in figuring out the best way to handle a disagreement or trading accusations about "not being a team player"; guided by this clearly defined process, people can devote their time and energy to exploring and constructively evaluating a variety of options for how to move forward. Intel's systematic method for working through differences has helped sustain some of the company's hallmark qualities: innovation, operational efficiency, and the ability to make and implement hard decisions in the face of complex strategic choices.

PROVIDE PEOPLE WITH CRITERIA FOR MAKING TRADE-OFFS

At our hypothetical Matrix Corporation, senior managers overseeing cross-unit sales teams often admonish those teams to "do what's right for the customer." Unfortunately, this exhortation isn't much help when conflict arises. Given Matrix's ability to offer numerous combinations of products and services, company managers—each with different training and experience and access to different information, not to mention different unit priorities—have, not surprisingly, different opinions about how best to meet customers' needs. Similar clashes in perspective result when exasperated senior managers tell squabbling team members to set aside their differences and "put Matrix's interests first." That's because it isn't always clear what's best for the company given the complex interplay among Matrix's objectives for revenue, profitability, market share, and long-term growth.

Even when companies equip people with a common method for resolving conflict, employees often will still need to make zero-sum trade-offs between competing priorities. That task is made much easier and less contentious when top management can clearly articulate the criteria for making such choices. Obviously, it's not easy to reduce a company's strategy to clearly defined trade-offs, but it's worth trying. For example, salespeople who know that five points of market share are more important than a ten point increase on a customer satisfaction scale are much better equipped to make strategic concessions when the needs and priorities of different parts of the business conflict. And even when the criteria do not lead to a straightforward answer, the guidelines can at least foster productive conversations by providing an objective focus. Establishing such criteria also sends a clear signal from management that it views conflict as an inevitable result of managing a complex business.

At Blue Cross and Blue Shield of Florida, the strategic decision to rely more and more on alliances with other organizations has significantly increased the potential for disagreement in an organization long accustomed to developing capabilities in-house. Decisions about whether to build new capabilities, buy them outright, or gain access to them through alliances are natural flashpoints for conflict among internal groups. The health insurer might have tried to minimize such conflict through a structural solution, giving a particular group the authority to make decisions concerning whether, for instance, to develop a new claims-processing system in-house, to do so jointly with an alliance partner, or to license or acquire an existing system from a third party.

Instead, the company established a set of criteria designed to help various groups within the organization—for example, the enterprise alliance group, IT, and marketing—to collectively make such decisions.

The criteria are embodied in a spreadsheet-type tool that guides people in assessing the trade-offs involved— say, between speed in getting a new process up and running versus ensuring its seamless integration with existing ones—when deciding whether to build, buy, or ally. People no longer debate back and forth across a table, advocating their preferred outcomes. Instead, they sit around the table and together apply a common set of trade-off criteria to the decision at hand. The resulting insights into the pros and cons of each approach enable more effective execution, no matter which path is chosen. (For a simplified version of the trade-off tool, see the exhibit "Blue Cross and Blue Shield: Build, Buy, or Ally?")

USE THE ESCALATION OF CONFLICT AS AN OPPORTUNITY FOR COACHING

Managers at Matrix spend much of their time playing the organizational equivalent of hot potato. Even people who are new to the company learn within weeks that the best thing to do with cross-unit conflict is to toss it up the management chain. Immediate supervisors take a quick pass at resolving the dispute but, being busy themselves, usually pass it up to *their* supervisors. Those supervisors do the same, and before long the problem lands in the lap of a senior-level manager, who then spends much of his time resolving disagreements. Clearly, this isn't ideal. Because the senior managers are a number of steps removed from the source of the controversy, they rarely have a good understanding of the

Blue Cross and Blue Shield: Build, Buy, or Ally?

One of the most effective ways senior managers can help resolve cross-unit conflict is by giving people the criteria for making trade-offs when the needs of different parts of the business are at odds with one another. At Blue Cross and Blue Shield of Florida, there are often conflicting perspectives over whether to build new capabilities (for example, a new claims-processing system, as in the hypothetical example below), acquire them, or gain access to them through an alliance. The company uses a grid-like poster (a simplified version of which is shown here) that helps multiple parties analyze the trade-offs associated with these three options. By checking various boxes in the grid using personalized markers, participants indicate how they assess a particular option against a variety of criteria: for example, the date by which the new capability needs to be implemented; the availability of internal resources such as capital and staff needed to develop the capability; and the degree of integration required with existing products and processes. The table format makes criteria and trade-offs easy to compare. The visual depiction of people's "votes" and the ensuing discussion help individuals see how their differences often arise from such factors as access to different data or different prioritizing of objectives. As debate unfolds—and as people move their markers in response to new information—they can see where they are aligned and where and why they separate into significant factions of disagreement. Eventually, the criteria-based dialogue tends to produce a preponderance of markers in one of the three rows, thus yielding operational consensus around a decision.

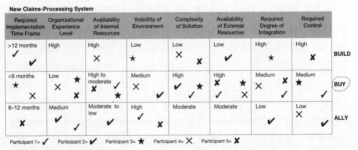

New Claims-Processing System

Required Implementation Time Frame	Organizational Experience Level	Availability of Internal Resources	Volatility of Environment	Complexity of Solution	Availability of External Resources	Required Degree of Integration	Required Control	
>12 months ✓ ✓	High ✕	High ✕	Low ★	Low ✕ ✗	Low ✓	High ★	High ✗	**BUILD**
<6 months ★ ✕	Low ✕ ★ ✗	High to moderate ✗ ✓ ★	Medium ✕ ✓	High ✓ ✗ ✓ ★	High ✕ ★ ✓ ✕	Medium ✕ ✗ ✓	Medium ★ ✓	(BUY)
6–12 months ✗	Medium ✓ ✓	Moderate to low ✓	High ✓ ✗	Moderate	Moderate	Low ✓	Low ✕ ✓	**ALLY**

Participant 1= ✓   Participant 2= ✔   Participant 3= ★   Participant 4= ✕   Participant 5= ✗

Source: Blue Cross and Blue Shield of Florida

situation. Furthermore, the more time they spend resolving internal clashes, the less time they spend engaged in the business, and the more isolated they are from the very information they need to resolve the disputes dumped in their laps. Meanwhile, Matrix employees get so little opportunity to learn about how to deal with conflict that it becomes not only expedient but almost necessary for them to quickly bump conflict up the management chain.

While Matrix's story may sound extreme, we can hardly count the number of companies we've seen that operate this way. And even in the best of situations—for example, where a companywide conflict-management process is in place and where trade-off criteria are well understood—there is still a natural tendency for people to let their bosses sort out disputes. Senior managers contribute to this tendency by quickly resolving the problems presented to them. While this may be the fastest and easiest way to fix the problems, it encourages people to punt issues upstairs at the first sign of difficulty. Instead, managers should treat escalations as opportunities to help employees become better at resolving conflict. (For an example of how managers can help their employees improve their conflict resolution skills, see the exhibit "IBM: Coaching for Conflict.")

At KLA-Tencor, a major manufacturer of semiconductor production equipment, a materials executive in each division oversees a number of buyers who procure

---

IBM: Coaching for Conflict

Managers can reduce the repeated escalation of conflict up the management chain by helping employees learn how to resolve disputes themselves. At IBM, executives get training in conflict

management and are offered online resources to help them coach others. One tool on the corporate intranet (an edited excerpt of which is shown here) walks managers through a variety of conversations they might have with a direct report who is struggling to resolve a dispute with people from one or more groups in the company—some of whom, by design, will be consulted to get their views but won't be involved in negotiating the final decision.

If you hear from someone reporting to you that . . .	The problem could be that . . .	And you could help your report by saying something like . . .
"Everyone still insists on being a decision maker."	The people your report is dealing with remain concerned that unless they have a formal voice in making the decision—or a key piece of the decision—their needs and interests won't be taken into account.	"You might want to explain why people are being consulted and how this information will be used." "Are there ways to break this decision apart into a series of subissues and assign decision-making roles around those subissues?" "Consider talking to the group about the costs of having everyone involved in the final decision."
"If I consult with this person up front, he might try to force an answer on me or create road blocks to my efforts to move forward."	The person you are coaching may be overlooking the risks of not asking for input—mainly, that any decision arrived at without input could be sabotaged later on.	"How would you ask someone for input? What would you tell her about your purpose in seeking it? What questions would you ask? What would you say if she put forth a solution and resisted discussing other options?" "Is there a way to manage the risk that she will try to block your efforts other than by not consulting her at all? If you consult with her now, might that in fact lower the risk that she will try to derail your efforts later?"
"I have consulted with all the right parties and have crafted, by all accounts, a good plan. But the decision makers cannot settle on a final decision."	The right people were included in the negotiating group, but the process for negotiating a final decision was not determined.	"What are the ground rules for how decisions will be made? Do all those in the group need to agree? Must the majority agree? Or just those with the greatest competence?" "What interests underlie the objective of having everyone agree? Is there another decision-making process that would meet those interests?"

the materials and component parts for machines that the division makes. When negotiating a companywide contract with a supplier, a buyer often must work with the company commodity manager, as well as with buyers from other divisions who deal with the same supplier. There is often conflict, for example, over the delivery terms for components supplied to two or more divisions under the contract. In such cases, the commodity manager and the division materials executive will push the division buyer to consider the needs of the other divisions, alternatives that might best address the collective needs of the different divisions, and the standards to be applied in assessing the trade-offs between alternatives. The aim is to help the buyer see solutions that haven't yet been considered and to resolve the conflict with the buyer in the other division.

Initially, this approach required more time from managers than if they had simply made the decisions themselves. But it has paid off in fewer disputes that senior managers need to resolve, speedier contract negotiation, and improved contract terms both for the company as a whole and for multiple divisions. For example, the buyers from three KLA-Tencor product divisions recently locked horns over a global contract with a key supplier. At issue was the trade-off between two variables: one, the supplier's level of liability for materials it needs to purchase in order to fulfill orders and, two, the flexibility granted the KLA-Tencor divisions in modifying the size of the orders and their required lead times. Each division demanded a different balance between these two factors, and the buyers took the conflict to their managers, wondering if they should try to negotiate each of the different trade-offs into the contract or pick among them. After being coached to consider how each division's business model shaped its preference—and using this understanding to jointly brainstorm alternatives—the buyers and commodity manager arrived at a creative solution that worked for everyone: They would request a clause in the contract that allowed them to increase and decrease flexibility in order volume and lead time, with corresponding changes in supplier liability, as required by changing market conditions.

Strategies for Managing Conflict upon Escalation

Equipped with common conflict resolution methods and trade-off criteria, and supported by systematic coaching, people are better able to resolve conflict on their own. But certain complex disputes will inevitably need to be decided by superiors. Consequently, managers must ensure that, upon escalation, conflict is resolved constructively and efficiently—and in ways that model desired behaviors.

ESTABLISH AND ENFORCE A REQUIREMENT OF JOINT ESCALATION

Let's again consider the situation at Matrix. In a typical conflict, three salespeople from different divisions become involved in a dispute over pricing. Frustrated, one of them decides to hand the problem up to his boss, explaining the situation in a short voice-mail message. The message offers little more than bare acknowledgment of the other salespeoples' viewpoints. The manager then determines, on the basis of what he knows about the situation, the solution to the problem. The salesperson, armed with his boss's decision, returns to his counterparts and shares

with them the verdict—which, given the process, is simply
a stronger version of the solution the salesperson had put
forward in the first place. But wait! The other two salespeople have also gone to *their* managers and carried back
stronger versions of *their* solutions. At this point, each
salesperson is locked into what is now "my manager's
view" of the right pricing scheme. The problem, already
thorny, has become even more intractable.

The best way to avoid this kind of debilitating deadlock is for people to present a disagreement jointly to
their boss or bosses. This will reduce or even eliminate
the suspicion, surprises, and damaged personal relationships ordinarily associated with unilateral escalation.
It will also guarantee that the ultimate decision maker
has access to a wide array of perspectives on the
conflict, its causes, and the various ways it might be
resolved. Furthermore, companies that require people
to share responsibility for the escalation of a conflict
often see a decrease in the number of problems that are
pushed up the management chain. Joint escalation
helps create the kind of accountability that is lacking
when people know they can provide their side of an issue
to their own manager and blame others when things
don't work out.

A few years ago, after a merger that resulted in a
much larger and more complex organization, senior
managers at the Canadian telecommunications company
Telus found themselves virtually paralyzed by a daily
barrage of unilateral escalations. Just determining who
was dealing with what and who should be talking to
whom took up huge amounts of senior management's
time. So the company made joint escalation a central
tenet of its new organizationwide protocols for conflict
resolution—a requirement given teeth by managers'

refusal to respond to unilateral escalation. When a conflict occurred among managers in different departments concerning, say, the allocation of resources among the departments, the managers were required to jointly describe the problem, what had been done so far to resolve it, and its possible solutions. Then they had to send a joint write-up of the situation to each of their bosses and stand ready to appear together and answer questions when those bosses met to work through a solution. In many cases, the requirement of systematically documenting the conflict and efforts to resolve it—because it forced people to make such efforts—led to a problem being resolved on the spot, without having to be kicked upstairs. Within weeks, this process resulted in the resolution of hundreds of issues that had been stalled for months in the newly merged organization.

ENSURE THAT MANAGERS RESOLVE ESCALATED CONFLICTS DIRECTLY WITH *THEIR* COUNTERPARTS

Let's return to the three salespeople at Matrix who took their dispute over pricing to their respective bosses and then met again, only to find themselves further from agreement than before. So what did they do at that point? They sent the problem *back* to their bosses. These three bosses, each of whom thought he'd already resolved the issue, decided the easiest thing to do would be to escalate it themselves. This would save them time and put the conflict before senior managers with the broad view seemingly needed to make a decision. Unfortunately, by doing this, the three bosses simply perpetuated the situation their salespeople had created, putting forward a biased viewpoint and leaving it to their own managers to come up with an answer. In the end, the decision was made unilaterally by the senior manager with the most organizational clout. This result bred resentment back down the management chain. A sense of "we'll win next time" took hold, ensuring that future conflict would be even more difficult to resolve.

It's not unusual to see managers react to escalations from their employees by simply passing conflicts up their own functional or divisional chains until they reach a senior executive involved with all the affected functions or divisions. Besides providing a poor example for others in the organization, this can be disastrous for a company that needs to move quickly. To avoid wasting time, a manager somewhere along the chain might try to resolve the problem swiftly and decisively by herself. But this, too, has its costs. In a complex organization, where many issues have significant implications for numerous parts of the business, unilateral responses to unilateral escalations are a recipe for inefficiency, bad decisions, and ill feelings.

The solution to these problems is a commitment by managers—a commitment codified in a formal policy—to deal with escalated conflict directly with their counterparts. Of course, doing this can feel cumbersome, especially when an issue is time-sensitive. But resolving the problem early on is ultimately more efficient than trying to sort it out later, after a decision becomes known because it has negatively affected some part of the business.

In the 1990s, IBM's sales and delivery organization became increasingly complex as the company reintegrated previously independent divisions and reorganized itself to provide customers with full solutions of bundled products and services. Senior executives soon recognized that managers were not dealing with escalated conflicts and that relationships among them were strained because they failed to consult and coordinate around cross-unit issues. This led to the creation of a forum called the Market Growth Workshop (a name carefully chosen to send a message throughout the company that getting cross-unit conflict resolved was critical to meeting customer needs and, in turn, growing market share). These monthly conference calls brought together managers, salespeople, and frontline product specialists from across the company to discuss and resolve cross-unit conflicts that were hindering important sales—for example, the difficulty salespeople faced in getting needed technical resources from overstretched product groups.

The Market Growth Workshops weren't successful right away. In the beginning, busy senior managers, reluctant to spend time on issues that often hadn't been carefully thought through, began sending their subordinates to the meetings—which made it even more difficult to resolve the problems discussed. So the company developed a simple preparation template that forced people to document and analyze disputes before the conference calls. Senior managers, realizing the problems created by their absence, recommitted themselves to attending the meetings. Over time, as complex conflicts were resolved during these sessions and significant sales were closed, attendees began to see these meetings as an opportunity to be involved in the resolution of high-stakes, high-visibility issues.

MAKE THE PROCESS FOR ESCALATED CONFLICT RESOLUTION TRANSPARENT

When a sales conflict is resolved by a Matrix senior manager, the word comes down the management chain

in the form of an action item: Put together an offering
with this particular mix of products and services at these
prices. The only elaboration may be an admonishment
to "get the sales team together, work up a proposal, and
get back to the customer as quickly as possible." The
problem is solved, at least for the time being. But the
salespeople—unless they have been able to divine
themes from the patterns of decisions made over time—
are left with little guidance on how to resolve similar
issues in the future. They may justifiably wonder: How
was the decision made? Based on what kinds of assumptions? With what kinds of trade-offs? How might the
reasoning change if the situation were different?

In most companies, once managers have resolved a
conflict, they announce the decision and move on. The
resolution process and rationale behind the decision are
left inside a managerial black box. While it's rarely helpful for managers to share all the gory details of their
deliberations around contentious issues, failing to take
the time to explain how a decision was reached and the
factors that went into it squanders a major opportunity.
A frank discussion of the trade-offs involved in decisions
would provide guidance to people trying to resolve conflicts in the future and would help nip in the bud the
kind of speculation—who won and who lost, which managers or units have the most power—that breeds mis-
trust, sparks turf battles, and otherwise impedes
cross-organizational collaboration. In general, clear communication about the resolution of the conflict can
increase people's willingness and ability to implement
decisions.

During the past two years, IBM's Market Growth
Workshops have evolved into a more structured
approach to managing escalated conflict, known as

Cross-Team Workouts. Designed to make conflict resolution more transparent, the workouts are weekly meetings of people across the organization who work together on sales and delivery issues for specific accounts. The meetings provide a public forum for resolving conflicts over account strategy, solution configuration, pricing, and delivery. Those issues that cannot be resolved at the local level are escalated to regional workout sessions attended by managers from product groups, services, sales, and finance. Attendees then communicate and explain meeting resolutions to their reports. Issues that cannot be resolved at the regional level are escalated to an even higher-level workout meeting attended by cross-unit executives from a larger geographic region—like the Americas or Asia Pacific—and chaired by the general manager of the region presenting the issue. The most complex and strategic issues reach this global forum. The overlapping attendance at these sessions—in which the managers who chair one level of meeting attend sessions at the next level up, thereby observing the decision-making process at that stage— further enhances the transparency of the system among different levels of the company. IBM has further formalized the process for the direct resolution of conflicts between services and product sales on large accounts by designating a managing director in sales and a global relationship partner in IBM global services as the ultimate point of resolution for escalated conflicts. By explicitly making the resolution of complex conflicts part of the job descriptions for both managing director and global relationship partner—and by making that clear to others in the organization—IBM has reduced ambiguity, increased transparency, and increased the efficiency with which conflicts are resolved.

Tapping the Learning Latent in Conflict

The six strategies we have discussed constitute a framework for effectively managing organizational discord,
one that integrates conflict resolution into day-to-day
decision-making processes, thereby removing a critical
barrier to cross-organizational collaboration. But the
strategies also hint at something else: that conflict can
be more than a necessary antecedent to collaboration.

Let's return briefly to Matrix. More than three-
quarters of all cross-unit sales at the company trigger
disputes about pricing. Roughly half of the sales lead to
clashes over account control. A substantial number of
sales also produce disagreements over the design of customer solutions, with the conflict often rooted in divisions' incompatible measurement systems and the
concerns of some people about the quality of the solutions being assembled. But managers are so busy trying
to resolve these almost daily disputes that they don't see
the patterns or sources of conflict. Interestingly, if they
ever wanted to identify patterns like these, Matrix managers might find few signs of them. That's because salespeople, who regularly hear their bosses complain about
all the disagreements in the organization, have concluded that they'd better start shielding their superiors
from discord.

The situation at Matrix is not unusual—most companies view conflict as an unnecessary nuisance—but that
view is unfortunate. When a company begins to see conflict as a valuable resource that should be managed and
exploited, it is likely to gain insight into problems that
senior managers may not have known existed. Because
internal friction is often caused by unaddressed strains
within an organization or between an organization and

its environment, setting up methods to track conflict and examine its causes can provide an interesting new perspective on a variety of issues. In the case of Matrix, taking the time to aggregate the experiences of individual salespeople involved in recurring disputes would likely lead to better approaches to setting prices, establishing incentives for salespeople, and monitoring the company's quality control process.

At Johnson & Johnson, an organization that has a highly decentralized structure, conflict is recognized as a positive aspect of cross-company collaboration. For example, a small internal group charged with facilitating sourcing collaboration among J&J's independent operating companies—particularly their outsourcing of clinical research services—actively works to extract lessons from conflicts. The group tracks and analyzes disagreements about issues such as what to outsource, whether and how to shift spending among suppliers, and what supplier capabilities to invest in. It hosts a council, comprising representatives from the various operating companies, that meets regularly to discuss these differences and explore their strategic implications. As a result, trends in clinical research outsourcing are spotted and information about them is disseminated throughout J&J more quickly. The operating companies benefit from insights about new offshoring opportunities, technologies, and ways of structuring collaboration with suppliers. And J&J, which can now piece together an accurate and global view of its suppliers, is better able to partner with them. Furthermore, the company realizes more value from its relationship with suppliers—yet another example of how the effective management of conflict can ultimately lead to fruitful collaboration.

J&J's approach is unusual but not unique. The benefits it offers provide further evidence that conflict—so often viewed as a liability to be avoided whenever possible—can be valuable to a company that knows how to manage it.

The Three Myths of Collaboration

COMPANIES ATTEMPT to foster collaboration among different parts of their organizations through a variety of methods, many based on a number of seemingly sensible but ultimately misguided assumptions:

Effective Collaboration Means "Teaming"

Many companies think that teamwork training is the way to promote collaboration across an organization. So they'll get the HR department to run hundreds of managers and their subordinates through intensive two- or three-day training programs. Workshops will offer techniques for getting groups aligned around common goals, for clarifying roles and responsibilities, for operating according to a shared set of behavioral norms, and so on.

Unfortunately, such workshops are usually the right solution to the wrong problems. First, the most critical breakdowns in collaboration typically occur not on actual teams but in the rapid and unstructured interactions between different groups within the organization. For example, someone from R&D will spend weeks unsuccessfully trying to get help from manufacturing to run a few tests on a new prototype. Meanwhile, people in manufacturing begin to complain about arrogant engineers from R&D expecting them to drop everything to help with another one of R&D's pet projects. Clearly, the need for collaboration extends to areas other than a formal team.

The second problem is that breakdowns in collaboration almost always result from fundamental differences among business functions and divisions. Teamwork training offers little guidance on how to work together in the context of competing objectives and limited resources. Indeed, the frequent emphasis on common goals further stigmatizes the idea of conflict in organizations where an emphasis on "polite" behavior regularly prevents effective problem solving. People who need to collaborate more effectively usually don't need to align around and work toward a common goal. They need to quickly and creatively solve problems by managing the inevitable conflict so that it works in their favor.

An Effective Incentive System Will Ensure Collaboration

It's a tantalizing proposition: You can hardwire collaboration into your organization by rewarding collaborative behavior. Salespeople receive bonuses not only for hitting targets for their own division's products but also for hitting cross-selling targets. Staff in corporate support functions like IT and procurement have part of their bonuses determined by positive feedback from their internal clients.

Unfortunately, the results of such programs are usually disappointing. Despite greater financial incentives, for example, salespeople continue to focus on the sales of their own products to the detriment of selling integrated solutions. Employees continue to perceive the IT and procurement departments as difficult to work with, too focused on their own priorities. Why such poor results? To some extent, it's because individuals think—for the most part correctly—that if they perform well in their own operation they will be "taken care of" by their bosses. In addition, many people find that the costs of working with individuals in other parts of the organization—the extra time required, the aggravation—greatly outweigh the rewards for doing so.

Certainly, misaligned incentives can be a tremendous obstacle to cross-boundary collaboration. But even the most carefully constructed incentives won't eliminate tensions between people with competing business objectives. An incentive is too blunt an instrument to enable optimal resolution of the hundreds of different trade-offs that need to be made in a complex organization. What's more, overemphasis on incentives can create a culture in which people say, "If the company wanted me to do that, they would build it into my comp plan." Ironically, focusing on incentives as a means to encourage collaboration can end up undermining it.

Organizations Can Be Structured for Collaboration

Many managers look for structural and procedural solutions—cross-functional task forces, collaborative "groupware," complex webs of dotted reporting lines on the organization chart—to create greater internal collaboration. But bringing people together is very different from getting them to collaborate.

Consider the following scenario. Individual information technology departments have been stripped out of a company's business units and moved to a corporatewide, shared-services IT organization. Senior managers rightly recognize that this kind of change is a recipe for conflict because various groups will now essentially compete with one another for scarce IT resources. So managers try mightily to design conflict out of, and collaboration into, the new organization. For example, to enable collaborative decision making within IT and between IT and the business units, business units are required to enter requests for IT support into a computerized tracking system. The system is designed to enable managers within the IT organization to prioritize projects and optimally deploy resources to meet the various requests.

Despite painstaking process design, results are disappointing. To avoid the inevitable conflicts between business units and IT over project prioritization, managers in the business units quickly learn to bring their requests to those they know in the IT organization rather than entering the requests into the new system. Consequently, IT professionals assume that any project in the system is a lower priority—further discouraging use of the system. People's inability to deal effectively with conflict has undermined a new process specifically designed to foster organizational collaboration.

Originally published in March 2005
Reprint R0503F

Lead from the Center

How to Manage Divisions Dynamically

MICHAEL E. RAYNOR AND JOSEPH L. BOWER

Executive Summary

CONVENTIONAL WISDOM HOLDS that a company's divisions should be given almost total autonomy—especially under conditions of uncertainty— because they are closer to emerging technologies, customers, and competitors than corporate headquarters could ever be. But research from Michael Raynor and Joseph Bower suggests that the corporate office should be more, not less, directive in turbulent markets.

Rapid changes in an industry make it difficult to predict where and when synergies among divisions might emerge. With so many possibilities and such uncertainty, companies can't afford to sacrifice their ability to flexibly execute business strategy. Corporate headquarters must play an active role in defining the scope of division-level strategy, the authors say, so that divisions do not act in ways that undermine opportunities to collaborate in the future. But neither can companies afford to sacrifice the competitiveness of their divisions as stand-alone businesses. In creating corporate-level strategic flexibility, a corporate office must balance the need for divisional autonomy now with the potential need for cooperation in the future.

Through an examination of four corporations—Sprint, WPP, Teradyne, and Viacom—the authors challenge traditional approaches to diversification in which a company's divisions are either related (they share resources and collaborate) or unrelated (they compete for resources and operate as stand alone businesses). They argue that companies should adopt a dynamic approach to cooperation among divisions, enabling varying degrees of relatedness between divisions depending on strategic circumstances. The authors offer four tactics to help executives manage divisions dynamically.

No ONE NEEDS convincing that in today's turbulent, competitive business environments corporations must be flexible and responsive. A host of forces are arrayed against even the most prescient strategist: technology, regulation, and globalization, to name only three. The question companies now face is not whether they need to be nimble and quick, but how.

Most of the advice on this score is remarkably consistent. Especially in large, complex, diversified companies, the prescription is "more decentralization"–at the limit, an almost complete devolution of decision-making authority to the operating divisions and those people closest to emerging technologies, competitors, and customers. This point of view has been espoused so often and with such conviction that one might even refer to it as the conventional wisdom.

Like most conventional wisdom, however, this approach does not always serve us well. We have found that responding effectively in uncertain markets often requires more–not less–direction from the center. Our research into contemporary diversified companies suggests that, in industries undergoing rapid and difficult-to-predict change, corporate headquarters must play an active role in defining the scope of division-level strategy. Furthermore, to compete effectively as a corporation, it often falls to the CEO and a select staff to drive the timing and nature of cooperative efforts between divisions.

The role of the corporate office in creating a strategically flexible organization has cascading effects on how executives manage other aspects of the company: whether divisions are clustered into groups, for example, and how compensation is structured. The result is a set of managerial challenges fundamentally different from those of diversified companies in more stable and slowly changing environments. Through an examination of four corporations–Sprint, WPP, Teradyne, and Viacom–we will explore the defining managerial characteristics of what it means to manage divisions dynamically.

The Sprint Story

The Sprint case illustrates the need for corporate-level strategic flexibility–and is an example of its successful implementation. Now a $20 billion telecommunications corporation, Sprint began life in 1901 as a rural Kansas telephone company. For the next 75 years, the company grew in traditional ways, acquiring other local telephone companies and vertically integrating into the manufacture and distribution of telecommunications equipment. Between 1976 and the mid-1990s, Sprint developed into a major diversified telecom player: it built a nationwide fiber-optic network, created a substantial long-distance business, entered the digital wireless business, took a minority stake in an Internet service provider, invested in broadband, and entered the Latin American, Western European, and Asian markets.

These businesses are at least nominally related, in that they all compete in the telecommunications industry. However, for much of its history, Sprint has had very few opportunities to capture meaningful synergies between its various businesses. For example, when Sprint moved into the long-distance market, it was unable to draw on expertise or assets from the local division, largely for regulatory reasons. Even ignoring regulation, the two businesses had little in common: they were based on different technologies, served different markets, and operated in different competitive contexts. That was the case for many of Sprint's new business initiatives, which functioned independently of one another despite their surface-level similarities.

As technological, regulatory, and market forces began to change, Sprint looked for ways to exploit synergies between its once autonomous divisions. Consider the evolving relationship between the local telephone division and the consumer long-distance division. In the wake of the Telecommunications Act of 1996, which, among other things, began to break down the barriers between the local and long-distance businesses, Sprint launched One Sprint, an initiative designed to expand the local phone business by selling the fullest possible range of Sprint services. Practically speaking, this meant finding ways to cross-sell long-distance service to local customers. Beginning in 1998, the local telephone and the consumer long-distance divisions cooperated to create bundled products; for a flat fee, Sprint's local customers could purchase local loop access, specialized dialing features, and blocks of long-distance time in configurations previously unavailable from the long-distance division.

The results speak for themselves. According to Sprint's executives, by the end of 1999 Sprint had achieved 27% consumer long-distance market share in areas in which Sprint was the local provider, compared with 7% market share in other areas. In fact, as the program gathered steam, during one 30-day period Sprint increased its market share by as much as 2%. Mike Fuller, CEO of the local business, says his group became the long-distance division's best distribution channel.

In this case, the benefits of integration were clear, and corporate headquarters did not have to twist arms to get the divisions to cooperate. It simply set targets for the local division based on developing new sources of revenue. The long-distance division, meanwhile, operated on the straightforward belief that any channel that profitably increases market share is a good channel.

In other cases, however, Sprint's corporate headquarters needed to take direct action to encourage cooperation among divisions. By doing so, Sprint was able to create and exploit corporate-level strategic flexibility.

Creating Flexibility

In creating strategic flexibility, a corporate office must balance the immediate need for divisional autonomy with the potential need for future cooperation. Without this balance, divisions may act in ways that advance their current competitiveness but undermine opportunities to collaborate in the future. The way in which Sprint approached wireless Internet access is an excellent example of how to achieve balance.

Launched in 1998, Sprint PCS was an extremely successful new entrant into the wireless market, signing on 4 million customers in its first full year of operation. When it decided to add wireless Internet service to its existing wireless telephone service in 1999, PCS's executives faced a critical decision: which software interface should it use for customer access to the Internet. (For various reasons–including the small size of the handsets–established Internet browsers like Netscape Navigator and Microsoft's Internet Explorer were not options.) The key question was how much flexibility should PCS give consumers: should they be able to customize their access software by, for example, choosing a home page and other settings? Or should Sprint hardwire those features? From the division's point of view, it was a no-brainer: give customers as many choices as possible. That would help the division gain market share and would probably make the new service profitable more quickly.

Corporate headquarters saw the problem differently. Taking a longer term, higher level perspective, the executives concluded that "owning" the interface between the customer and the network trumped the immediate appeal of growing market share quickly by appealing to customers' interest in openness. They foresaw a time in the not-too-distant future when they'd want a common platform for various emerging products–narrowband, broadband, wireline, wireless, and so on. As a result, they overruled Sprint PCS's executives. Even though there were no definite plans for integration, Sprint's corporate office created flexibility by constraining the activities of its fastest-growing division. Had Sprint given PCS complete freedom to pursue its own course–one that made perfect sense in isolation–it could have undermined the scope of activities that the larger organization might pursue in the future. Strategic constraints of the kind Sprint imposed here are critical if a diversified corporation is to be genuinely flexible.

The use of strategic constraints should not be confused with routine intervention by a corporate office. To create strategic flexibility, divisions must still enjoy considerable operational autonomy and remain competitive as stand-alone businesses. Companies must walk a thin line–something Sprint's corporate executives seem to have accomplished. In the PCS example, corporate executives imposed constraints on the division, but in other cases, the corporate office adopted a hands-off approach. Consider the following example, in which a division made major operational changes with only minimal oversight.

When the executives of Sprint's consumer long-distance division thought their "dime a minute" marketing platform was getting stale–partly because its long-time spokesperson, Candice Bergen, was no longer starring in a popular television show–they wanted to lower their prices and make some other brand-altering decisions. Len Lauer, then president of the division, and his team developed the "nickel nights" concept, and Lauer ran it by Sprint's COO, Ron LeMay. The two

executives spent all of 30 minutes together, and then
Lauer's team was free to launch the new identity of the
consumer long-distance company–and cut the price of
its core product in half. The only constraint imposed
was that the new program had to meet rate-of-return
hurdles established by the finance staff to ensure that
the company met its EVA targets. Determining the right
market objectives–and the pricing tactics to meet those
objectives–was the exclusive purview of the operating
division.

The kind of operational autonomy that Sprint's consumer long-distance organization enjoyed in this case
demonstrates that a division must be a successful stand-
alone business in its own right, rather than being dependent for success on future integration with other
divisions. Corporate-level strategic flexibility is not
merely staged integration, and the increasing interde-
pendence of operating divisions is never a foregone con-
clusion. Instead, divisional autonomy is combined with
strategic constraints to ensure that strong
businesses–competitive in their own right–have the ability to integrate when and if the opportunity arises.

Exploiting Flexibility

The goal, then, is to make sure the company is in a
position to move nimbly when opportunities for integration emerge. The way Sprint, for example, bundled its
consumer long-distance and wireless services provides
insight into the demands that exploiting strategic
flexibility places on the corporate office.

Recall that Sprint PCS had been launched in 1998
and that its revenues and market share were growing
extremely quickly. For the consumer long-distance

division, the PCS business represented an invaluable opportunity to sell Sprint long distance: by bundling long distance with the popular wireless offering, the division could gain valuable market share.

The consumer long-distance marketing group was enthusiastic about exploiting Sprint PCS's distribution channels, but PCS's managers strongly resisted the idea. One reason was that the sales process for PCS services is a long and expensive one: it can take up to 90 days and four visits before a customer signs the contract. An integration initiative that merely tacked on consumer long-distance services to existing PCS offerings would run the risk of corrupting PCS's sales process, thereby undermining the very growth that the long-distance group sought to leverage.

It was a PCS product technologist who found a possible way out of that impasse. He came up with a plan to integrate long-distance and wireless services and increase the attractiveness of the PCS offering—in a way that promised to double the long-distance division's gross margin and improve customer value. His approach, which was dubbed "block of time lite," or BOTL, was based on PCS's model of selling blocks of time—100, 200, 500, 1,000 minutes per month—for a set fee. The sticking point in the typical sales process was that customers felt one plan didn't provide enough talk time, but the next offering provided too much. The new BOTL plan would allow customers to use the minutes for either long-distance or PCS services. This shift would mitigate customer concerns about over- or underbuying and let the long-distance group charge ten cents (rather than the now-standard five cents) a minute.

Whatever the theoretical attractiveness of this product offering, however, PCS's executives still resisted it vigorously. Their division was growing fast, and their compensation was linked to meeting targets developed long before this approach was proposed. Introducing products that might upset PCS's well-oiled and rapidly expanding distribution systems was legitimately viewed as a risky undertaking.

The corporate office saw the strategic value in the integration and intervened to allay the PCS division's various concerns. PCS's executives were worried, for example, that the long-distance business's high level of churn would increase their own churn. Tom Weigman, an executive vice president who'd been president of the consumer long-distance division before assuming a corporate role, tackled the churn debate at a very detailed level, developing a plan to roll out the bundled service in several test markets. PCS's executives also argued that introducing the BOTL plan so late in the year (it was slated for trial in the fourth quarter of 1999) would make PCS miss its operating targets. Al Kurtze, then an executive vice president in Sprint's corporate office and formerly the COO of Sprint PCS, stepped in and demonstrated how the new product tests could be rolled out without endangering targets for that fiscal year. As a result of the corporate office's efforts, BOTL was launched in test markets in 1999. It took the detailed, top-down involvement of the corporate executives to persuade division leaders that placing strategic constraints on the fast-growing division would improve competitiveness in the long run.

Another aspect of exploiting flexibility is to have malleable compensation structures that can reflect rapid changes in the degree of interdivisional cooperation. Sprint's management incentive program–which pays division presidents annual cash bonuses of up to 100% of their base salaries–certainly does that. No division president has more than 65% percent of the bonus dependent on his or her division's performance. The remaining 35% to 50% depends on the performance of other divisions, thereby providing an incentive to search for synergies. When Sprint believes that a potential synergy is ready for exploitation, it builds that belief into the compensation structure, resulting in dramatic swings in the allocation of bonus payments. For example, bonus payments tied to cross-selling initiatives can change by as much as 300% in a single year, accounting for 30% of the total incentive bonus payment.

Dynamic Thinking About Diversification

Sprint exemplifies many of the defining characteristics of strategic flexibility (see the exhibit "Characteristics

---

Characteristics of Corporate-Level Strategic Flexibility

Companies create flexibility by balancing the competing demands of divisional autonomy in the present with divisional cooperation in the future. They exploit flexibility by moving nimbly when opportunities for cooperation emerge.

Phase	Defining Characteristics
Creating	• Build a portfolio of businesses between which valuable synergies are possible, now or in the future • Ensure that divisions have sufficient autonomy to develop business models and succeed as stand-alone entities • Impose strategic boundaries to ensure that future integration remains possible • Reward search activity
Exploiting	• Promote integration opportunities when they are expected to be profitable to the company as a whole • Engage division-level resistance • Change reward systems to reflect the importance of interdivisional cooperation

of Corporate-Level Strategic Flexibility). These characteristics lay the groundwork for a dynamic approach to
managing corporate strategy at diversified corporations.

Any framework for thinking about corporate strategy is
built on an understanding of how divisions interact with
one another and how they interact with the corporate
office. If divisions share valuable resources or capabilities,
we take it as evidence of a strategy of related diversification. In such cases, the relationship between headquarters
and divisions is structured to facilitate interdivisional
cooperation. Divisions with related operations are often
organized in groups, headed by corporate-level executives
responsible for managing synergies between divisions
within their groups. Alternatively, if divisions compete for
resources or capabilities, we take that as evidence of unrelated diversification. Division-level executives lead the
organizations as stand-alone businesses; the corporate
office typically exerts strong financial oversight but rarely
intervenes in divisional affairs.

What is remarkable about Sprint is that the company
doesn't conform to either model. Nor is it making the
transition from unrelated to related diversification
(though this is what an observer might assume). Instead,
Sprint is doing something new that calls into question
several assumptions that have long been central to conventional thinking about the management of diversified
organizations. Let's look at how several other companies
are challenging those assumptions and exploring new
territory.

The first assumption is that diversification strategy
must be either related or unrelated. But many companies
are finding that some objectives are best pursued with
stand-alone divisions and others with cooperating
divisions.

This is precisely the approach Martin Sorrell has taken as CEO of WPP, the world's largest marketing services firm. Over the past 15 years, Sorrell has created a collection of professional services firms that includes three of the largest ad agencies in the world–J. Walter Thompson, Ogilvy & Mather, and Young & Rubicam–as well as public relations, corporate identity, market research, and specialty ad firms. His goal: to provide soup-to-nuts marketing services to large clients. In the pursuit of that goal, somewhat counterintuitively, Sorrell's structural moves have created unrelated, freestanding divisions. To sustain strong performance, a powerful finance and treasury staff has introduced the controls and incentive systems one expects to find in an unrelated diversifier.

At the same time, Sorrell has taken steps to encourage cooperation among stand-alone units. As at Sprint, incentive compensation and a stock program are managed to encourage cooperation. Most intriguing, perhaps, are WPP's "virtual companies." These organizations have essentially no staff–a CEO and an assistant at most–and no offices. One, the Common Health, became the world's biggest health care marketing services firm with just a single employee–the CEO. For each project, the CEO would assemble a team from an ever-shifting alliance of subsidiaries, selecting the right capabilities to respond to each client's needs.

Yet even the virtual companies, built on a model of strong interdivisional cooperation, have structures and processes that resemble those of an unrelated diversifier. The virtual companies have no income statement; profit and loss is calculated by project and allocated to the participating subsidiaries. Compensation is based on subsidiary performance and, to a significant extent, one's career develops in a given subsidiary.

WPP's approach demonstrates that it is possible to pursue varying degrees of relatedness among divisions. That is, some divisions are tightly linked, others operate in a more loosely allied way, while others are entirely stand-alone. Moreover, at WPP, the degree of relatedness waxes and wanes depending upon strategic circumstances. Relatedness is sought only when the professionals within freestanding businesses believe that they can serve their clients better by achieving it.

A second assumption of traditional thinking is that only business units–not the corporate office–create value for the company. But we've found the corporate office can create value by assembling a portfolio of assets and capabilities that will drive competition in the future–and managing those assets in a flexible way so as not to hinder the ability of the divisions to compete now. Although the performance results show up in better competitiveness at the business-unit level, the seeds of the success–the value creation–reside in the forward-looking actions of the corporate office.

Consider how the CEO of Teradyne, a manufacturer of chip-testing equipment, created new value by fostering an emerging technology in the face of divisional resistance. Through the mid-1990s, Teradyne's primary product line consisted of highly engineered, very expensive testers sold to manufacturers of microprocessors. Each division had separate manufacturing facilities and a separate P&L; they competed for budget and capital and were compensated based on divisional performance. However, they all sold and serviced their products through a single global organization.

In the early 1990s, CEO Alex d'Arbeloff realized that new chip technology and advances in software might make a smaller, more flexible tester possible. When none of the divisions would allocate the talent necessary to develop this potentially disruptive technology, d'Arbeloff intervened. He established a start-up subsidiary that reported outside the regular control system to an internal board of directors. As the product developed, he insisted that the subsidiary make regular briefings to the other divisions to share knowledge of the new technology. When new customers (minicontroller manufacturers) embraced the tester–turning it into a hit–the sales force rallied around what had been an ugly duckling. Existing divisions recognized the need and opportunity to cooperate with the new division and began to adapt the new chip and software technology.

If the corporate office can generate value by creating a forward-looking portfolio, it follows that headquarters needs to influence division-level decisions, especially those that might lead to interdivisional cooperation. Stated simply, there is a clear role for selective top-down, detail-oriented corporate management. And so crumbles the third and final assumption about diversification–that corporate-divisional relationships are driven exclusively by the needs of the divisions.

Global media giant Viacom illustrates the benefits of an activist corporate office. In 1998, Paramount, Viacom's movie studio, was negotiating European distribution agreements with the Kirsch Group, the leading German media conglomerate. With a \$1 billion offer on the table, Paramount was anxious to close the deal. But MTV and Nickelodeon (both part of Viacom) also wanted to establish positions in the German market. Viacom's president encouraged the divisions to develop a collective position, and division managers spent several months at the end of 1998 attempting, but failing, to do so. Early in 1999, Sumner Redstone, Viacom's chairman and majority share-owner, intervened directly. He traveled to Europe, met with many of the key players in the German market, and developed an auction for the Paramount films. Several media companies, including Kirsch, bid on the distribution rights. When the contract was finally signed, it was for $2 billion–and it included access for both MTV and Nickelodeon.

Like the executives at Sprint, WPP, and Teradyne, Redstone intervened based on his unique corporate-level understanding of the value of synergies between divisions and the singular power of the corporate office to effect integration quickly. When he took action, he was careful not to undermine the principles of decentralized operating authority that governed the divisions, which

---

Two Approaches to Managing Diversified Companies

Conventional wisdom assumes that divisions are either related or unrelated and that new value is created only at the business-unit level. New thinking, however, offers a dynamic approach to cooperation among divisions, through direct action by the corporate office.

Static Thinking

Diversification strategy is either related or unrelated; interdivisional relationships are static.

Corporate value is created exclusively at the business-unit level.

Corporate-divisional relationships are driven exclusively by business-unit needs.

Dynamic Thinking

Diversification strategy can be a mixture of related and unrelated elements; companies can pursue varying degrees of relatedness between divisions. The degree of relatedness waxes and wanes depending upon strategic circumstances.

Corporate value is also created at the strategic level: portfolio structure can create shareholder value.

Corporate-divisional relationships are significantly affected by corporate-level strategic considerations.

the company continued to value. However, Redstone, like all these executives, understood that long-term strategic integration requires selective, top-down intervention by the corporate office from time to time.

The differences between the more static view of diversification and the dynamic approach described here are summarized in the exhibit "Two Approaches to Managing Diversified Companies." This comparison reveals that, where traditional thinking was comparatively rigid, the new thinking is aligned with the dynamic needs of corporate-level strategic flexibility.

Preparing for Dynamic Moves

The companies that will benefit most from a dynamic approach to corporate strategy are those operating in highly uncertain competitive environments in which, despite the uncertainty, the need to make significant portfolio-level investments remains. It is no accident that the companies profiled here come from just such environments. At Sprint, competing successfully in the wireless business meant moving quickly to secure spectrum licenses and investing billions in infrastructure. If WPP was to include the marquee advertising brands in its stable, it had to acquire those businesses when they became available. And Teradyne's new business development efforts had to proceed at least as quickly as the underlying technology evolved.

In each case, portfolio diversification preceded the integration efforts, which had always been a part of the original strategic intent. Forced to diversify before meaningful synergies can be captured, flexible corporations must maintain the competitiveness of each individual business. To do so, they rely on the strict financial controls and the divisional autonomy typically seen in more static, unrelated diversified companies. At the same time, if future integration is to remain a possibility, the corporate office must impose strategic constraints, lest complete independence lead to the pursuit of division-level strategies that undermine possible future synergies. Coping with the disconnect between expanding the corporation's portfolio and integrating divisions in pursuit of synergy requires the adoption of four management tactics.

COMBINE STRICT FINANCIAL CONTROLS WITH A FLEXIBLE STRUCTURE

The powerful financial controls and planning associated with traditional diversified companies must be in place to ensure that individual businesses maintain strong performance results. However, a conventional group structure is likely to be inappropriate. Group structures typically make it more difficult for the corporate office to identify and assess the full range of possible cross-divisional opportunities. Moreover, interdivisional cooperation is usually hardwired by the structure, limited to divisions in the same group. Group structures also tend to make it more difficult for corporate line leadership–not financial or planning staff–to communicate regularly with operating business managers about strategic questions. A more flexible structure, coupled with tight financial controls, best serves a dynamic corporate strategy. Compensation structures, too, must be flexible enough to support frequent and significant changes in strategic priorities.

BE A PLAYER

If corporate leaders are going to contribute to the substance of strategy, they need to be informed. That means being out in the market and in touch with customers, regulators, competitors, Wall Street analysts, and even academics. At Sprint, CEO Bill Esrey was a key player in Washington as the telecommunications debate evolved. At Teradyne, Alex d'Arbeloff kept himself informed about cutting edge technology through an active role in the venture capital community, extensive volunteer activities at MIT, and regular attendance at industry meetings. Sumner Redstone is notorious in his company for talking to anyone and everyone about the issues he believes are important.

HAVE A LEAN BUT POWERFUL CORPORATE OFFICE

For all the corporate-level activity, the corporate office supporting a dynamic strategy should be relatively small. With the exception of finance and human resources, most staff positions should remain in the divisions. The executives in the corporate office are there to help the CEO; they usually have worked closely with the CEO in the past and gained his or her trust. Their importance lies in their judgment, not in their formal roles. At Sprint, the two corporate executives charged with driving inter-divisional cooperation had extensive operating experience at the company. Each was supported by a staff of two or three people at most. These few executives formed a kitchen cabinet rather than a structured corporate staff with assigned responsibilities.

SPEND TIME ON STRATEGY

Divisional executives can't waste time when they are with the CEO. Monthly or quarterly reviews of operations are necessary, but the focus of the executive meetings has to be the strategic opportunities that markets offer, regardless of divisional lines. In addition to formally scheduled meetings, corporate and division executives should have frequent conversations that are not cluttered up with operational issues. Operating executives at Sprint and Viacom speak of being on the phone with their CEOs often. Martin Sorrell uses e-mail to stay in constant touch with his operating executives–and most anyone else who writes him.

Creating a truly dynamic corporate strategy goes far beyond merely attempting to combine various existing approaches. It is not enough for the corporate office to be by turns directive and standoffish. Nor should it attempt to be both simultaneously. Rather, dynamic corporate strategy is something fundamentally different that brings with it a host of new management challenges. As the forces of change impinge ever more sharply on an increasing range of industries, we expect that more and more diversified companies will benefit from thinking–and acting – in ways that create and exploit corporate-level strategic flexibility.

Managing Divisions in Stable versus Uncertain Markets

THE NEED FOR STRATEGIC FLEXIBILITY in some companies does not render traditional frameworks for thinking about managing diversified companies invalid in all competitive contexts. Those that will benefit the most from strategic flexibility are companies operating in uncertain markets. But many well-managed and respected diversified corporations will continue to conform to traditional approaches for the simple reason that they remain entirely appropriate.

Consider, for example, AlliedSignal. Acquired by Honeywell in 2000, which in turn was acquired by GE in 2001, AlliedSignal was a creature of the diversification wave of the late 1970s and early 1980s. Under the leadership of Larry Bossidy from 1991 to 2000, AlliedSignal was a paragon of the multibusiness enterprise, and there was very little about the organization that suggested the kind of strategic flexibility that characterizes Sprint, WPP, Teradyne, and Viacom.

For instance, AlliedSignal made extensive use of a group structure; corporate-level executives were responsible for managing synergies between divisions within their groups. Consequently, the company had an aerospace group, a plastics group, a chemicals group, and so on. Although grouping divisions in this way improves the information-processing capacity of the organization as a whole, it can also restrict the interactions between divisions that are not in the same group. The imposition of a hierarchical structure serves to filter information, embed patterns of communication in reporting relationships, and make it more difficult for managers to see and act upon opportunities for cooperation between operating units. In a sense, then, a traditional group structure serves to hardwire the nature of the possible links within a diversified corporation.

This was a small price to pay for AlliedSignal, since there was very little uncertainty or variability in the nature of interdivisional relationships. Simply put, it was unlikely that the Prestone antifreeze division in the consumer products group would have much to offer the engine systems division in the aerospace group, so the increased efficiency of the group structure more than outweighed the cost of any lost flexibility.

At Sprint, by contrast, rapid changes in the telecommunications industry continue to make it difficult to predict where and when key linkages might emerge. There are potentially compelling arguments to be made for grouping long distance with local service or bundling wireless access with long-distance service or integrating local service with wireless access, and so on. With so many possibilities and such uncertainty, Sprint cannot afford to sacrifice its flexibility in execution, and so the company has avoided imposing a group structure. Consequently, all of Sprint's operating divisions report directly to the corporate office.

Compensation systems also reinforce either traditional or flexible diversification strategies. The compensation systems at AlliedSignal reflected the stability of the relationships between its divisions. The compensation of managers whose divisions were operationally linked was tied to their joint performance. Compensation structures for operating units that had no material links with other operating units contained no interunit components. That approach is in stark contrast to Sprint's compensation system, in which every division's compensation is tied to every other unit regardless of whether links actually exist.

When it came to exploiting synergies at AlliedSignal, corporate executives typically exerted pressure on the divisions, but operating managers chose how to respond to that pressure. In other words, in keeping with traditional management thinking, the corporate office took advantage of its broader view to press for more synergies where appropriate, but it respected the more detailed knowledge of those closest to the work and the customers. Similarly, strategy formulation at AlliedSignal required the corporate office to provide financial targets but relied on operating managers to develop specific initiatives to meet those targets.

Comparing Traditional and Flexible Corporate Management Systems

Traditional Systems for a Stable Business Environment	**Flexible Systems for a Rapidly Changing Business Environment**
Extensive use of group structure	Little or no use of group structure
Stable compensation systems linked to existing interdivisional synergies	Rapidly changing compensation systems that reward cooperative behavior, even if there are no current linkages
Integration efforts typically identified by senior management but designed and implemented by operating management	Integration efforts identified and designed to a large degree by corporate management over the active resistance of operating management
The corporate office guides the formulation of strategy by imposing financial constraints	The corporate office guides the formulation of strategy by imposing strategic constraints

At Sprint, both of those processes work quite differently. Operating divisions are subject to strategic constraints as part of their strategy formulation process. This serves to *create* flexibility. But, to *exploit* that flexibility, division managers must take more than passing notice of the detailed input provided by corporate executives.

Originally published in May 2001
Reprint R0105F

Silo Busting

How to Execute on the Promise of Customer Focus

RANJAY GULATI

In 2001, under price pressure from the government and managed health care organizations, GE Medical Systems (now GE Health-care) created a unit, Performance Solutions, to sell consulting services packaged with imaging equipment as integrated solutions. These solutions, priced at a premium, were intended to enhance productivity by, for instance, reducing patient backlogs. At the time, lots of companies were making the move from selling products to selling solutions in an attempt to differentiate themselves in increasingly commoditized markets.

GE's plan seemed to work well at first. The Performance Solutions unit enjoyed strong initial revenues, in part because most new contracts included additional consulting services valued at $25,000 to $50,000. And the unit had some notable successes. It helped Stanford University Medical Center, for example, make the transition to an all-digital imaging environment at its adult hospital, children's medical center, and an outpatient facility—moves that delivered millions of dollars in new revenues for the medical center and substantial cost savings.

But by 2005, the unit's growth had begun a swift decline. It turned out that equipment salespeople had trouble explaining the value of consulting services, so when they called on customers they couldn't contribute much to the sale of additional services. What's more, these reps were reluctant to allow Performance Solutions salespeople to contact their customers. And by marketing the unit's consulting services with its product portfolio, GE generated solutions that were useful for customers whose problems could clearly be solved using GE's equipment but less compelling for those whose needs were linked only loosely to the imaging products.

In the end, GE refashioned the unit to address customers' needs in a more comprehensive fashion and to better align the sales organization. For instance, the majority of solutions now focus mainly on consulting services and are no longer marketed only with GE equipment. The solutions group secured new contracts valued at more than $500 million in 2006. But in trying to escape the perils of commoditization, the company initially fell into a classic trap: It was seeking to solve customer problems but was viewing those problems through the lens of its own products, rather than from the customer's perspective. It was pulling together what it had on offer in the hope that customers would value the whole more than the sum of its parts.

Over the past five years, I have studied the challenge of top- and bottom-line growth in the face of commoditization, and I have found that many companies make the same mistake. They profess the importance of shifting from products to solutions—in fact, in a survey of senior executives I conducted a few years ago, more than two-thirds of the respondents cited this shift as a strategic priority in the next decade. But their knowledge and expertise are housed within organizational silos, and they have trouble harnessing their resources across those internal boundaries in a way that customers truly value and are willing to pay for.

Some notable exceptions have emerged: companies that, like GE, found ways to transcend those silos in the interest of customer needs. By the late 1990s, for instance, Best Buy had nearly saturated the market with store openings and was facing increased competition not just from other retailers like Wal-Mart but from suppliers such as Dell. It tried to spark growth through various marketing approaches, but the company's efforts didn't take off until it launched a major initiative to restructure around customer solutions. Between 2000 and 2005, Best Buy's stock price grew at an annual rate of almost 30%.

Commercial real estate provider Jones Lang LaSalle (JLL), under serious price competition, made a similar strategic shift in 2001, when its large customers began demanding integrated real estate services. For instance, corporate customers wanted the same people who found or built property for them to manage it. In response, JLL adopted a solutions-oriented structure that helped attract numerous large and highly profitable new accounts.

For GE Healthcare, Best Buy, and JLL, as well as for other companies I have studied, the journey to understand and unite around customer needs was a multiyear endeavor with major challenges and setbacks along the way. The effort required systematic, ongoing change to help organizations transcend existing product-based or geographic silos and, in some cases, replace them with customer-oriented ones. In particular, I found that successful companies engaged in four sets of activities:

Coordination. Establishing structural mechanisms and processes that allow employees to improve their focus on the customer by harmonizing information and activities across units.

Cooperation. Encouraging people in all parts of the company—through cultural means, incentives, and the allocation of power—to work together in the interest of customer needs.

Capability development. Ensuring that enough people in the organization have the skills to deliver customer-focused solutions and defining a clear career path for employees with those skills.

Connection. Developing relationships with external partners to increase the value of solutions cost effectively.

The first three sets of activities mutually reinforce the effort to put customers at the organization's fore; the fourth dramatically increases the power and reach of solutions by focusing attention beyond the firm's boundaries. All of them help companies transcend internal silos in service of higher-value customer solutions.

Coordination for Customer Focus

As GE Healthcare quickly discovered, it's easy to say that you offer solutions; salespeople may readily seize the concept as their newest product. But I've found that few companies are actually structured to deliver products and services in a synchronized way that's attractive from a customer's perspective. Individual units are historically focused on perfecting their products and processes, and give little thought to how their offerings might be even more valuable to the end user when paired with those of another unit. It's not just that the status quo doesn't reward collaborative behavior—although the right incentives are also critical. It's that the connections literally aren't in place.

One way to forge those connections is to do away with traditional silos altogether and create new ones organized by customer segments or needs. Many companies, however, are understandably reluctant to let go of the economies of scale and depth of knowledge and expertise associated with non-customer-focused silos. A company organized around geographies can customize offerings to suit local preferences, for instance, while a technology-centric firm can be quick to market with technical innovations. In many cases, functional and geographic silos were created precisely to help companies coordinate such activities as designing innovative products or gaining geographic focus. A customer focus requires them to emphasize a different set of activities and coordinate them in a different way.

In their initial attempts to offer customer solutions, companies are likely to create structures and processes that transcend rather than obliterate silos. Such boundary-spanning efforts may be highly informal—even as simple as hoping for or encouraging serendipity and impromptu conversations that lead to unplanned cross-unit solutions. But the casual exchange of information and ideas is generally most effective among senior executives, who have a better understanding than their subordinates of corporate goals and easier access to other leaders in the organization.

One way to achieve more-formal coordination without discarding existing silos is to layer boundary-spanning roles or units over the current structure and charge them with connecting the company's disparate activities to customer needs. JLL, which was created by the 1999 merger of LaSalle Partners and Jones Lang Wootton, had organized the corporate side of its business in the Americas into three units, each offering a particular service: representing tenants who wished to lease or purchase, maintaining buildings and properties, and managing real estate development. Each unit had authority over what services to offer, at what price, and to which clients. The units also had profit-and-loss responsibility for their respective businesses.

In 2001 the firm began to hear complaints from such large corporate clients as Bank of America that buying real estate services piecemeal from numerous companies and interacting with relatively junior salespeople were taking up too much executive time. One client explained, "We like him [the ad hoc account manager], but he is too low on the totem pole." At the time, many *Fortune* 500 companies were starting to outsource all real estate management. In response, JLL created an umbrella group, Corporate Solutions, that comprised the three service units as well as an account management function, which served as a point of contact for large corporate customers. The account management group was staffed with high-ranking officers who had the authority to negotiate the pricing and delivery of real estate solutions, and the experience to help clients with strategic planning. By approaching Bank of America with a dedicated, senior-level account manager, JLL addressed the customer's complaint and was rewarded with one of just two spots (reduced from five) as a provider of outsourced services for the bank's 65 million square feet of U.S. real estate. Thus began a tremendous run that saw JLL's solutions revenue in the Americas grow more than 50% between 2002 and 2005.

Cisco Systems took a similar, layered approach to customer focus, but with a twist. The company, which had been organized by customer segment from 1997 to 2001, reverted to a technology-focused structure after the Internet bubble burst, forcing the company to address costly redundancies. Under its previous structure, Cisco had been creating the same or similar products for different customer segments, whose needs often overlapped. In fact, in some cases each line of business offered its own technology or solution for the same problem.

However, leaders feared that organizing around technologies, which involved centralizing marketing and R&D, would distance Cisco from customers' requirements. The answer was to retain the company's three sales groups based on customer type but establish a central marketing organization—residing between the technology groups and the customer-facing sales units—responsible for, among other things, facilitating the integration of products and technologies. The marketing group also established a cross-silo solutions-engineering team to bring disparate technologies together in a lab, test them, and create blueprints for end-user solutions. In addition to those structural measures, Cisco implemented several customer-focused processes, such as a customer champion program, which assigned senior executives as advocates for important customers. CEO John Chambers, for instance, was designated Ford's champion in 2002. In 2004 the company supplemented its advocates with cross-functional leadership teams organized by customer type, mimicking the previous structure, at least at the senior management level. Those teams—described by one executive as "the voice of the customer"—oversee six end-to-end processes that cut across functional boundaries such as quote-to-cash (the order cycle) and issue-to-resolution (technical support).

While bridging mechanisms such as cross-silo teams and processes can be very effective, they aren't easy to implement. A history of independence often leads to protectionist behavior. At JLL, for instance, business unit managers were initially reluctant to cede decision-making authority to account managers, particularly ones who lacked experience with that unit's service. Conflicts also arose over pricing and account managers' compensation. What's more, while JLL's Corporate Solutions group had positioned the firm well to meet the increasing demands of corporate real estate customers, single-transaction customers considered the relatively small number of JLL account managers in local markets to be a problem. Those customers wanted professionals who could negotiate the best deal and execute entire transactions. As JLL discovered, the benefits of bundled solutions wear off if customers perceive a weakness in any component. Ultimately, JLL's layered approach to silo busting was still limiting the firm's growth.

To dispense with such tensions, JLL next took the more dramatic and highly formal measure of silo swapping—a wholesale, permanent structural shift to spin internal groups and processes around a customer axis. That is, it swapped its current, service-focused silos for those structured explicitly around the customer to maximize company-customer synergies. As part of that process, it replaced the account management function and the three service silos that had resided within the Corporate Solutions group with two organizations denoted simply Clients and Markets, a restructuring that put more people in the field, closer to clients, and focused all internal groups and processes on customer needs. The Markets organization handled one-off transactions, represented JLL's full range of offerings to those customers, and provided local support for larger clients. As accounts grew, they were assigned an account manager from the Clients organization, which was composed primarily of account teams managing the firm's relationships with large, multiservice customers. These teams were considered profit centers and so had the authority to hire and terminate employees. To preserve its product and service expertise without a product- and service-based structure, JLL embedded service specialists within account teams in both organizations and created a product management team charged with keeping offerings competitive. It's too soon to know how well the customer-focused silos are working, and the firm may face new, unanticipated challenges, but early results look promising: In the past year, revenues have increased by 30% and profits by almost 60%.

Culture of Cooperation

While coordination mechanisms can align tasks and information around customers' needs, they don't necessarily inspire a willingness among members of competing silos to fully cooperate and make sometimes time-consuming and costly adjustments in the interest of customers. Just as important as coordination, then, is a cooperative environment in which people are rewarded for busting through silos to deliver customer solutions. Customer-centric companies live by a set of values that put the customer front and center, and they reinforce those values through cultural elements, power structures, metrics, and incentives that reward customer-focused, solutions-oriented behavior.

Many product-centric companies probably start out with a focus on customers, aiming to design products with broad appeal. But after early successes, they internalize and institutionalize the notion that markets respond primarily to great products and services. Decisions and behaviors, including those related specifically to customers, are then viewed through the lens of the product. Quality, for example, is defined by meeting internal standards rather than customer requirements. Over time, even the sales and marketing departments lose their customer focus, as product successes dominate company lore. In this way, the company develops a pervasive inside-out perspective.

In contrast, customer-focused companies, even those in technology-intensive arenas, build an outside-in perspective into all major elements of their cultures. They hold solving customer problems above all else and celebrate customer-oriented victories. At Cisco, technical innovation is clearly valued. The drive to solve customer problems fuels that innovation no matter where it leads the company, a mind-set that is reflected in the statement on all employee badges, "No Technology Religion." As one manager said, "Being able to listen carefully to create relevancy [for customers] is a more important business value than innovation." In line with this thinking, Cisco puts a relatively large number of employees in direct contact with customers, including groups such as human resources that typically don't interact with customers.

It helped that Cisco had the luxury of an existing culture of customer focus. Cofounder Sandy Lerner, in the company's earliest days, invented a customized multiprotocol router for a customer who initially found no Cisco products that met his needs. From then on, Lerner made it her mission to establish a culture where everybody, even those in units distant from customers, went beyond providing standard customer support to addressing specific problems. Consequently, even when the company reorganized its silos away from the customer in 2001, it was able to maintain enough interaction among units to ensure a customer-centric view.

At least half the battle of promoting cross-silo, customer-focused cooperation lies in the "softer" aspects of culture, including values and the way the company communicates them through images, symbols, and stories. Touting service accomplishments instead of, or at least in addition to, product accomplishments through company lore can begin to shift people's mindsets. Cisco's employee badges broadcast a focus on customer needs, as does a well-known company legend about how Chambers was 30 minutes late to his first board meeting because he chose to take a call from an irate customer. Linguistic conventions may also be used to signify the value of the customer: Target and Disney refer to customers as "guests."

Another admittedly soft but powerful cultural tool for aligning employees around customer needs is to treat your workers the way you want them to treat customers. The hope is that people will adopt a collaborative orientation and customer focus because they want to, not just because they'll reap a financial reward. Cisco is highly egalitarian, reinforcing the notion that all employees are important, which makes them more likely to cooperate across silos. The company offers equal access to parking spaces, for instance, and designates window-facing cubicles for nonmanagement employees, locating supervisors' offices within the interior of the floor.

Of course, the softer cooperation-promoting measures won't take hold if the harder ones—power structures, metrics, and incentives—don't reinforce them. Power structures are notoriously difficult to change. For example, in a customer-centric environment, people who are close to the customer and adept at building bridges across silos should gain power and prominence; but unit leaders responsible for products or geographies who had clout in the old organization won't hand over their customer relationships and concomitant power bases without a struggle.

That was the case at JLL. Before the company created the Corporate Solutions organization, power resided almost exclusively within the service-based business units. Even after the account manager position was instituted, final pricing authority rested with the units, which made it difficult to compete with multiservice packages. Although solutions ideally carry a premium price, JLL's initial intent was to better serve customers' needs by simplifying the management of real estate and to position the firm as a multiservice provider. However, when JLL created a package of real estate services, the price quickly mounted, resulting in sticker shock among potential customers, many of whom associated buying in bulk with discount pricing. JLL unit heads—who wanted to maximize their own return, not subsidize other units—refused to budge on prices. In some cases, package proposals were delayed, thanks to negotiations that stalled or ended in a stalemate that could be resolved only by those higher in the organization. In other cases, the packages weren't priced competitively, and the firm lost the business.

The issue of autonomy raised concerns as well. JLL's business units were accustomed to a high degree of independence. They protected their client relationships and had always been wary of introducing other services— even before the account management unit was in place—because delivery would be out of their control and they feared damaging the relationships. JLL took several steps to resolve those tensions. For one, it signaled the importance and value of the account manager role by assigning it to only very senior executives, including two who had achieved the title of international director, a distinction earned by less than 2% of employees. The firm also delivered a series of presentations at annual company-wide meetings highlighting the significance of the role to the firm's growth.

To ease the pricing standoffs, JLL began in 2003 to allow account managers to provide input into the performance evaluations of business unit employees who touched their clients. At the same time, JLL took steps to retain some power and recognition for the business unit CEOs and, in the process, help them learn more about the services outside their silos and how they might gain personally from cross-unit sales. Unit CEOs, for example, were asked to oversee accounts on which their services were a particularly important component; in this role, unit heads were explicitly responsible for the performance of account managers. Because their bonuses were tied to the account managers' overall performance, the unit heads developed a clearer picture of the value contributed by services outside their silos. They were also required to meet regularly with customers to discuss their needs and the quality of the firm's service.

To support a shifting power landscape, firms must also embrace new metrics and incentives. The product-focused metrics most companies rely on—revenues, growth, and margins—don't reward cross-silo cooperation or customer centricity. Sales commissions in some organizations encourage managers to bring in new customers rather than nurture existing relationships, for example.

Cisco is relentless about measuring and rewarding employees on the basis of customer-related performance indicators. A Web-based survey helps determine the pre- and post-sale satisfaction of customers who buy directly from Cisco or indirectly through resellers. Survey questions focus on a customer's overall experience with and perceptions of Cisco, along with product-specific issues. Follow-up surveys with some customers explore their experiences with certain products more deeply. All bonuses are tied directly to these customer satisfaction data, so employees are encouraged to cooperate across internal boundaries. Moreover, all employees, including interns and part-timers, are eligible for stock options.

Building Capability

Regardless of the incentives and cultural elements in place to enhance customer-focused silo busting, employees will fall back on their old competencies and ways of thinking if they haven't developed new skills. For example, even though one of the companies I studied told product salespeople to include new consulting-based offerings in their pitches to customers, the reps found it easier to give a superficial account of the new offerings or to omit them from their pitches altogether. Old habits die hard.

As a company becomes more adept at inducing coordination and cooperation across units, new skills become valued and desirable. Rather than highly specialized expertise, customer-focused solutions require employees to develop two kinds of skills: multidomain skills (the ability to work with multiple products and services, which requires a deep understanding of customers' needs) and boundary-spanning skills (the ability to forge connections across internal boundaries). Such generalist skills are typically not rewarded or developed in a product-oriented organization, so it's not easy to find customer-facing generalists. The companies that succeed invest significant time and resources in developing generalists. Furthermore, they map clear career paths for those who pursue this route.

At JLL, most of the first account managers had spent the majority of their careers in a single service unit within the firm and remained members of that unit even after becoming account managers. Consequently, they were not always deeply acquainted with the other businesses or able to manage service bundles skillfully. Account managers hired from the outside were generally chosen for their ability to execute real estate transactions, not for the breadth of their service knowledge.

To foster the development of boundary-spanning skills and cultivate a cadre of employees who could grow into the account manager role, JLL began to rotate individuals through the three remaining silos (before swapping the service silos for customer silos), forcing them to acquire greater knowledge of the products, services, and capabilities of each unit, as well as to expand their personal networks across the firm. For those already in account management roles, the company instituted training sessions through regular conference calls and meetings. Early sessions tackled relatively simple tasks, such as the establishment of a common vocabulary. Subsequent sessions focused on improving account managers' knowledge of each unit's offerings and on cross-silo sales skills and new metrics, including the first rudimentary client-based profit-and-loss statements. An unanticipated benefit of the training was that it brought the account managers together regularly, helping them to stop identifying only with their silos and to begin forming a group identity that enhanced their cross-silo networks. As a natural consequence, top management could see that account managers were assuming increased responsibility for a broader range of services.

Best Buy's shift to solutions selling entailed identifying and targeting five large, profitable customer segments: young, tech-savvy adults; busy and affluent professionals; family men; busy, suburban moms; and small-business customers. Each store was designed to suit the needs of its largest customer segment. A "busy mom" store, for instance, features personal shopping assistance and a kid-friendly layout. Stores targeting the tech-savvy offer higher-end consumer electronics and separate showrooms for high-definition home theater systems. When the company rolled out its customer-centric strategy, it conducted extensive training to help employees understand their store's particular customer segment. It also trained sales associates on basic financial metrics to highlight how their efforts on behalf of target customers affect store performance.

At the corporate level, Best Buy created a Customer Centricity University for senior officers who had not been involved with planning the new strategy. For those executives, Best Buy outlined the rationale for the new approach, including detailed financials, and held breakout sessions with the teams responsible for developing and executing the strategy for each customer segment. Over 11 months, all employees and contractors residing at headquarters, as well as many other corporate employees, participated in the program. It was then disbanded, its essential elements incorporated into the company's orientation program for new employees.

Enhancing skill sets is only part of the challenge of capability building. Companies must also develop attractive career paths that give emerging generalist stars a sense of identity and a clear route for advancement. Even specialists whose roles may not change much in the new organization will probably have to develop some generalist skills and learn how these could contribute to their advancement. JLL, for instance, at first had difficulty attracting candidates for account manager positions, largely because the firm had measured success and offered promotions on the basis of achievements within a unit. Job security was a major concern for potential account managers, as one of the first to hold the position explains: "One of the big fears was that these accounts don't last forever. So if a person left his or her specialized area of expertise to run an account and after three years…the firm was no longer providing services for that account, employees feared that that person would be out of a job."

JLL addressed the career path issue in part through its customer-focused reorganization—whereby the Clients group housed account managers in a well-defined unit with a clear career trajectory. Other firms have developed "talent marketplaces" to signal the value they place on generalist, cross-silo skills. Modeled after informal marketplaces used within law firms, academia, and R&D units, these forums match employees on a flexible basis with available positions or assignments, thereby allowing generalist and specialist career tracks to coexist.

Connection with External Partners

The three factors we've discussed—coordination, cooperation, and capability building—are silo-busting tactics that align business units around a customer axis. But by redefining the boundaries of the company itself, firms can further fight commoditization in two ways: cutting costs by outsourcing all but core activities (and, in some cases, by finding creative ways to outsource them) and joining forces with companies that have complementary offerings to create even higher-value solutions, which command a larger price premium. Such approaches still require cross-boundary efforts, but the boundaries are between a company and its partners.

Starbucks continues to charge a premium for coffee, previously a commodity product, and exponentially increase the company's sales through intercompany relationships that keep costs low while expanding the firm's offerings. It chooses suppliers very carefully (quality and service take priority over cost) and then shares an unusual amount of financial information, using a two-way, open-book costing model that allows suppliers to see the company's margins and Starbucks to review the vendors' costs. In return, the company expects suppliers to treat it as a preferred customer in terms of pricing, profit percentage, and the resources committed to the partnership.

As for expanding its offerings, Starbucks seeks to enrich the customer experience through alliances with partners in a variety of industries. Its bottled Frappuccino beverage is manufactured, distributed, and marketed through a 50/50 joint venture with PepsiCo; its ice cream is made and distributed by Dreyer's; its supermarket coffees are marketed and distributed by Kraft, one of the company's main competitors in the at-home coffee consumption market. A more recent alliance with Jim Beam Brands brought Starbucks into a new drink category: spirits. In 2005, the two companies launched Starbucks Cream Liqueur, which is sold in liquor stores, restaurants, and bars, but not in coffeehouses.

Starbucks's boundary-expanding moves have extended to nonconsumable items as well. For several years, customers have been able to buy CDs at the stores, and the company recently began to promote movies as part of its ongoing efforts to become, according to the *New York Times,* a "purveyor of premium-blend culture." It sponsors discussion groups (with free coffee) and is considering selling DVDs, publishing new authors, and producing films. To coordinate these promotions and partnerships, Starbucks has formed an entertainment division with offices in Seattle and Los Angeles.

Finally, Starbucks has expanded internationally by leveraging not other companies' products and services but the capabilities of regional partners. Whereas the company owns most of its domestic retail stores, it allows foreign companies to own and operate Starbucks stores in markets where those players are already established. In 1995 Japanese specialty retailer Sazaby opened a Starbucks in Tokyo. In such cases, Starbucks provides operating expertise and control through licensing, while the foreign partners take on financial risk and advise Starbucks on real estate, regulations, suppliers, labor, and culture in the markets they know best. Sharing responsibilities in this way requires Starbucks to apply the principles of coordination, cooperation, and capability building to its external relationships.

Starbucks's relationship-building capability has enabled the company to grow far faster than it could have on its own. What's more, with just about every fast-food company selling premium coffee, and versatile and affordable new coffee-makers lining the shelves at Target, the company has been able to shore up its position by selling not just coffee but a coffeehouse experience, built largely around a series of partnerships and alliances that provide customers with an array of high-quality offerings.

Such relationships can be mutually reinforcing: As one company shrinks operations to cut costs—seeking partners to take on formerly in-house activities—its suppliers must expand their horizons by increasing the range of their offerings or finding their own partners to help them do this. IBM, even while taking over major back-office operations for large companies, has condensed its own core operations by outsourcing activities like repair and server manufacturing to contractors such as Solectron. Solectron, in turn, has expanded its boundaries by acquiring an IBM repair center in the Netherlands, allowing IBM to condense still further.

There are pitfalls to integrating closely with suppliers. Some companies—especially those that are unclear on their core values—give away too much. Others become captive to their key suppliers and lose the motivation to make ongoing investments in new technology. Some also find that they are funding the development expertise and scale that may allow a partner to become a competitor, as when cell phone supplier BenQ moved from making handsets for Motorola to marketing its own brand of handsets in foreign markets where Motorola already had a presence. Integrated partnerships can also be risky if companies put a lot of information into their vendors' hands, as Starbucks does. If trust on either side is eroded, one party could misuse the information.

In managing external relationships to avoid such pitfalls, it makes sense to apply the principles used to manage across internal silos—particularly the principles of coordination and cooperation. The challenges of internal and external execution are not exactly the same, but they share many themes, such as the need to find efficient ways of exchanging information and aligning incentives. So, for instance, Starbucks has a set of formal coordination structures to help information flow between partners. In addition to regular meetings between senior management on both sides, Starbucks has a dedicated training program for employees who will be involved in managing supplier relationships. To ensure that both parties follow clear rules for knowledge sharing, the company has created a handbook for suppliers, which describes the firm's purchasing philosophies and policies, along with the standards vendors must meet on eight criteria.

Cooperation issues may be even more central to external relationships than to internal ones, given the need to apportion value fairly among parties and the omnipresent risk of opportunistic behavior. Cultural fit lays the groundwork for cooperation, and efforts at cultural synchrony may begin even before the partnership does. Starbucks not only conducts a careful assessment of a supplier's brand and operations but also evaluates cultural fit, largely through an event called Discovery Day, when prospective partners come to Seattle to discuss cultural and other commonalities as well as differences between themselves and Starbucks.

In today's ever expanding and shifting business arena, and in light of a growing focus on customer needs, the definitions of what is inside a company and what is outside are no longer clear. But as our sense of firm boundaries evolves, so will our understanding of how best to breach internal and external barriers.

There are few downsides to developing true solutions. The risk is that in the rush to stand out in the crowd, many companies forget that solving customer problems requires a deep knowledge of who their target customers are and what they need. Some customers are better off purchasing products and services piecemeal. Leaders at GE Healthcare originally targeted solutions at large national accounts—which, it turned out, bought largely on price. These clients almost by definition weren't good candidates for the solutions offering. The company consequently refined its target customer profile to focus on multihospital systems—with at least $500 million in annual revenue—that demonstrated a willingness to provide GE with meaningful access to the most-senior executives. Through this targeting, GE Healthcare narrowed its focus to just 150 of the roughly 400 multihospital systems in the U.S. health care market—giving primary attention to 50 accounts that included customers ready to enter into a contractual relationship with GE and those that exhibited many key characteristics and expressed a willingness to work with GE.

The lesson for GE, as for others, is that it doesn't pay to put the solutions cart before the horse of coordinated customer focus. To stand out in a commoditized market, companies must understand what customers truly value. The only way to do that is to break down the traditional, often entrenched, silos and unite resources to focus directly on customer needs.

The Four Cs of Customer-Focused Solutions

COMPANIES LOOKING TO GROW in a commoditized marketplace like to say that they offer customer solutions: strategic packages of products and services that are hard to copy and can command premium prices. But most companies aren't set up to deliver solutions that customers truly value. Successful companies make significant changes in four areas to deliver real solutions.

Coordination.

In most companies, knowledge and expertise reside in distinct units—organized by product, service, or geography. To deliver customer-focused solutions, companies need mechanisms that allow customer-related information sharing, division of labor, and decision making to occur easily across company boundaries. Sometimes this involves completely obliterating established silos and replacing them with silos organized around the customer, but more often it entails using structures and processes to transcend existing boundaries.

Cooperation.

Customer-centric companies use both substance and symbolism to foster a culture of customer-focused cooperation. They develop metrics that measure, for instance, customer satisfaction and incentives that reward customer-focused behavior, even if it sacrifices unit performance. Most also shake up the power structure so that people who are closest to customers have the authority to act on their behalf.

Capability.

Delivering customer-focused solutions requires at least some employees to have two kinds of generalist skills. The first is experience with more than one product or service, along with a deep knowledge of customer needs (multidomain skills), and the second is an ability to traverse internal boundaries (boundary-spanning skills). In many companies, especially those organized around products, employees aren't rewarded for being generalists. Organizations that succeed in delivering solutions, however, invest significant time and resources in developing generalists. Furthermore, they establish clear career pathways for those who pursue the generalist route.

Connection.

By redefining the boundaries of the company in order to connect more tightly with external partners, companies can not only cut costs by outsourcing all but core activities (and perhaps even by finding ways to outsource them) but also create higher-value solutions by combining their offerings with those of a complementary partner. Working with other companies still means crossing boundaries, but in this instance the boundaries are between a company and its partners.

Originally published in May 2007
Reprint R0705F

Introducing T-Shaped Managers

Knowledge Management's Next Generation

AND BOLKO VON OETINGER

Executive Summary

MOST COMPANIES DO A POOR JOB of capitalizing on the wealth of expertise scattered across their organizations. That's because they tend to rely on centralized knowledge-management systems and technologies. But such systems are really only good at distributing explicit knowledge, the kind that can be captured and codified for general use. They're not very good at transferring implicit knowledge, the kind needed to generate new insights and creative ways of tackling business problems or opportunities.

The authors suggest another approach, something they call *T-shaped management*, which requires executives to share knowledge freely across their organization (the horizontal part of the "T"), while remaining fiercely committed to their individual business unit's performance (the vertical part).

A few companies are starting to use this approach, and one–BP Amoco–has been especially successful. From BP's experience, the authors have gleaned five ways that T-shaped managers help companies capitalize on their inherent knowledge. They increase efficiency by transferring best practices. They improve the quality of decision making companywide. They grow revenues through shared expertise. They develop new business opportunities through the cross-pollination of ideas. And they make bold strategic moves possible by delivering well-coordinated implementation.

All that takes time, and BP's managers have had to learn how to balance that time against the attention they must pay to their own units. The authors suggest, however, that it's worth the effort to find such a balance to more fully realize the immense value of the knowledge lying idle within so many companies.

Despite their best efforts, most companies continue to squander what may be their greatest asset in today's knowledge economy: the wealth of expertise, ideas, and latent insights that lies scattered across or

deeply embedded in their organizations. And that's
a shame, because capitalizing on those intellectual
resources—using existing knowledge to improve performance or combining strands of knowledge to create
something altogether new—can help companies respond
to a surprising array of challenges, from fending off
smaller, nimbler rivals to integrating businesses shoved
together in a merger.

Many companies have tried, with mixed success,
to leverage this underused asset by centralizing knowledge management functions or by investing heavily in
knowledge management technology. We suggest another
approach, one that requires managers to change their
behavior and the way they spend their time. The
approach is novel but, when properly implemented,
quite powerful.

We call the approach *T-shaped management*. It relies
on a new kind of executive, one who breaks out of the
traditional corporate hierarchy to share knowledge freely
across the organization (the horizontal part of the "T")
while remaining fiercely committed to individual business unit performance (the vertical part). The successful
T-shaped manager must learn to live with, and ultimately thrive within, the tension created by this dual
responsibility. Although this tension is most acute for
heads of business units, any T-shaped manager with
operating unit obligations must wrestle with it.

You might ask, Why rely so heavily on managers to
share knowledge? Why not just institute a state-of-the-
art knowledge management system? The trouble is that,
while those systems are good at transferring explicit
knowledge—for example, the template needed to perform a complicated but routine task—direct personal
contact is typically needed to effectively transfer implicit

knowledge—the kind that must be creatively applied
to particular business problems or opportunities and is
crucial to the success of innovation-driven companies.[1]
Furthermore, merely moving documents around can
never engender the degree of collaboration that's needed
to generate new insights. For that, companies really
have to bring people together to brainstorm.

Effective T-shaped managers will benefit companies
of almost any size, but they're particularly crucial in large
corporations where operating units have been granted
considerable autonomy. Although giving business units
greater freedom generally increases accountability, spurs
innovation, and promotes sensitivity to local market conditions, it also can lead to competition between units,
which may hoard, rather than share, expertise. By encouraging collaboration, a T-shaped management system can
be a powerful counterbalance to such negative behavior.

Our research over the past six years suggests that few
companies have recognized T-shaped management as
a key to success and even fewer have enjoyed its benefits.
So how do you successfully cultivate T-shaped managers
and capitalize on the value they can create?

Energy giant BP Amoco—a sprawling enterprise
with over 100,000 employees and operations in 100
countries—provides some provocative answers. Our
in-depth examination of BP's management practices,
including interviews with more than 25 business-unit
and corporate managers, highlighted five specific types
of value that T-shaped managers can generate. BP's
experience also suggests guidelines for creating an
environment in which T-shaped managers will flourish.
Such guidelines are important because the benefits
of T-shaped management won't be realized—will even
become liabilities—if the concept is poorly implemented.

A key insight: senior executives must put in place mechanisms that simultaneously promote and discipline managers' knowledge-sharing activities.

BP's Evolving Approach

The story of BP's ongoing effort to create an effective T-shaped management system is instructive in part because of a number of initial missteps the company made along the way. Indeed, the entire history of the T-shaped manager at BP is one of continually fine-tuning the tension between the manager's horizontal and vertical roles, an evolution that continues to this day.

The seeds of BP's T-shaped management approach were planted in the early 1990s at the oil and gas exploration division of what was then British Petroleum. In a successful bid to cut out layers of management and improve performance and financial accountability, the division—known as BPX and headed at the time by BP's current chief executive, John Browne—was divided into nearly 50 semiautonomous business units. But because business unit leaders were personally accountable for their units' performance, they focused primarily on the success of their own businesses rather than on the success of BPX as a whole.

With the ultimate aim of making BPX more valuable than the sum of its business units' results, Browne and his executives set out to encourage greater understanding of the goals and challenges of other units and of BPX as a whole. Early in 1992, they established "peer groups," in which leaders of roughly a dozen business units engaged in similar types of businesses met to discuss the strategic and technical challenges they all faced. The important thing about these meetings was that senior management wasn't allowed in the room. That reduced posturing and encouraged candor.

But over time, BPX's senior management realized that simply sharing knowledge for knowledge's sake— the creation of "learning loops," as one executive put it— was only marginally productive. So in 1994, the peer groups became more results oriented, assuming responsibility for allocating capital resources among business units in the group and for setting unit performance targets. In both cases, the aim was to further the broader interests of the entire peer group and help it meet its own goals, which were set by the BPX executive committee.

Not surprisingly, this approach initially caused considerable friction among the business unit leaders. "People were very combative about why their pet project merited investment," recalls John Leggate, who ran several BPX business units during this period. "But over time, and with some due process instituted within the groups, business unit leaders gradually became less partisan and thought about the bigger result." In fact, the unit heads began to see the benefits of this collaborative approach, including the opportunity to tap the knowledge and expertise of other units.

In 1995, when Browne became BP's CEO, he rolled out this system of collaboration and networking across the entire company. Since then, BP has become known for its knowledge-sharing practices.[2] Less known is BP's realization that, despite the clear benefits of such a system, you can overdo it.

For instance, BP had encouraged the formation not only of peer groups but also of cross-unit networks focused on areas of shared interest. Over time, this idea flowered into an unforeseen number of networks and subnetworks (the "helicopter utilization network" was one), which consumed increasing amounts of managers' time. An audit within BPX alone identified several hundred of these networks. "People always had a good reason for meeting," says Leggate, who is now BP's group vice president for digital business. "You're sharing best practices. You're having good conversations with like-minded people. But increasingly, we found that people were flying around the world and simply sharing ideas without always having a strong focus on the bottom line." So the company again tightened the reins, reducing the number of networks and limiting cross-unit meetings to those concerned with specific business results.

Technology has played a role in these knowledge-sharing activities. BP has an electronic "yellow pages" that identifies experts in different areas. And the company early on developed sophisticated digital-networking capabilities, such as multimedia e-mail and desktop videoconferencing, which enable managers to gather and work across business units in virtual teams. But technology has its limits. The expert directory quickly falls out of date and often fails to fully capture exactly what each person knows. And executives say that well-developed relationships, nurtured through face-to-face interaction, are fundamental to successful virtual teams.

As shortcomings have emerged, BP has modified its knowledge-sharing system. One sign of the system's strength has been its ability to function even as BP undertook the mammoth task of integrating the disparate cultures of two acquired rivals: Amoco in 1998 and ARCO last year. "The real value of mergers lies in the scope they offer for learning from a wider base of experience," says Browne. "We've begun to do that and, as we live through the process, we see more and more potential. Still, the process of leveraging the learning is itself a learning experience." The leap in scale and global presence that resulted from the mergers, for instance, has prompted BP to reorganize business units into new groups more strategically focused than the former peer groups. The evolution will continue, executives say, as strengths and weaknesses of the new system appear.

The T-Shaped Manager in Action

To get an idea of how BP's system works in practice, let's take a detailed look at an individual T-shaped manager.[3] David Nagel, BP's gas business unit head in Egypt, joined the company as a result of the Amoco merger and quickly found a key difference between his former and current employers. "Before, if you needed help in a particular area, you'd go to Houston for assistance," he says, referring to the former headquarters of Amoco's oil and gas business. Today, Nagel typically seeks help from his peers in other business units and often reciprocates, as well.

Like all BP business unit managers, Nagel has a two-part job description. He is effectively CEO of his business unit, with profit-and-loss, balance sheet, capital expenditure, and other responsibilities. These are spelled out in a personal annual performance contract he has with his boss, one of BP's group vice presidents. At the same time, Nagel is expected to engage in a variety of cross-unit knowledge-sharing activities, which he estimates consume somewhere between 15% and 20% of his time.

To ensure that his horizontal activities don't undermine the goal of outstanding unit performance, Nagel must carefully manage his time and energy. (See the exhibit "A T-Shaped Work-week.") That means continual self-monitoring to be sure that cross-unit activities in fact serve an important business purpose. "We've tried to eliminate the peer group meetings that are held just for the purpose of saying, 'We had a peer group meeting,'" Nagel says. "We recently canceled one that made sense when we scheduled it but that doesn't make sense anymore because the issues have changed."

A T-Shaped Workweek

A typical workweek for David Nagel, BP's gas business unit head in Egypt, shows how he balances his vertical (business unit) and horizontal (knowledge-sharing) responsibilities. (The workweek in Cairo runs from Sunday through Thursday.)

SUNDAY, OCTOBER 22

AM
- Egypt gas business-unit team meeting: progress versus the performance contract

PM
- Meet with UK representative from Barclays Bank
- Meet with UK government trade mission to Egypt
- **Team meeting with Egypt oil business unit leader on safety, commercial deals, and government and public relations**
- Note to fellow board members of local community services association (which provides services to expatriate BP employees) on simplified accounting practices

MONDAY, OCTOBER 23

AM
- Meet with Egyptian gas utility (partner on new project)

PM
- Chair Egyptian Petroleum Industry Environmental Protection Committee meeting
- **Meet with BP oil traders from London regarding opportunities in Egypt**

TUESDAY, OCTOBER 24

AM
- Meet with BP project management leader in Cairo to discuss new approach to project management in Egypt
- Check roles and responsibilities on BP emergency plans for Egypt
- Conference call with BP downstream organization (refined products and retailing) about opportunities in Egypt

PM
- Career discussion with gas unit staff members
- LNG (liquefied natural gas) project review
- **Review financial projections for peer group**
- **Seek peer input via e-mail on next steps for key project**

WEDNESDAY, OCTOBER 25

AM
- Fly to London; review business unit correspondence

PM
- **Peer group teleconference on financial submissions, upcoming meeting agenda**
- **Meet BP Algeria oil business unit leader (peer group member) to discuss future production opportunities**

THURSDAY, OCTOBER 26

AM
- **Peer assist to Algeria gas business unit**
- E-mails on business unit promotions, individual development plans

PM
- **Discussion with Spanish gas and power business unit leader on LNG opportunities**
- Fly to Cairo; review speech for upcoming BP GasTech Conference in Houston

FRIDAY, OCTOBER 27

AM/PM
- **Finalize peer group performance submissions for 2001**

KEY
- Business unit activities
- **Cross-unit activities**

The dual demands also have required him to delegate some business unit responsibilities, particularly gas exploration and production, to two trusted lieutenants. That frees him for tasks extending beyond his business unit.

The ones that involve knowledge sharing can be characterized quite simply: in a broad corporate context, Nagel collaborates, connects, gives, and takes.

He *collaborates* in a peer group comprising his business unit and seven others throughout the Mediterranean and Atlantic regions that, like his, are focused on increasing gas production. In fact, he is the facilitator of the group, responsible for convening the meetings and working to move its members toward agreement on the often thorny and challenging issues of exactly how to allocate capital and meet those peer-group production targets set by his division's executive committee. In September, the group determined, based on each unit's projections, that it was likely to fall about 3% short of its goal for 2001. Through some intense discussion over the course of the next two meetings, the group determined which business units were in the best position to close that gap.

Nagel also occasionally *connects* people from different parts of the company. For example, he may get a call from a legacy BP engineer seeking the name of a legacy Amoco engineer who could offer advice in an area in which Amoco was known to have particular strengths.

Nagel *gives* advice to other business units, when requested by individuals both within his peer group and beyond it. Last year, he and his managers were involved in roughly 20 such "peer assists" to other BP units; Nagel was personally involved in three of them.

And Nagel *takes* advice from other units. Last year, his business unit benefited from roughly ten peer assists, in which people came from around the world to offer specific ideas on such issues as his unit's marketing plan. Sometimes the help comes more informally. Shortly after the merger, an engineer in Nagel's unit tapped into his network of BP contacts and determined within several days that the productivity of a particular type of well being drilled in Egypt could be tested without "flaring" it—that is, without opening it up and burning off some gas. This allowed speedy evaluation of the well while avoiding environmental concerns about flaring that had arisen unexpectedly.

Why didn't Nagel seek help from headquarters, as he might have done at Amoco? "The model here is an open market of ideas," he says. "People develop a sense of where the real expertise lies. Rather than having to deal with the bureaucracy of going through the center, you can just cut across to somebody in Stavanger [Norway] or Aberdeen [Scotland] or Houston and say, 'I need some help. Can you give me a couple of hours?' And that is expected and encouraged."

Creating Horizontal Value

T-shaped managers like David Nagel create vertical value for BP in the form of strong business unit results—a top managerial priority at a company that emphasizes business unit accountability. They create horizontal value in one of five distinct ways, which progress up the value-added ladder from the exploitation of existing resources and knowledge to the exploration of new opportunities. The benefits at the lower end stem from traditional knowledge transfer; those at the upper end require collaboration to create new ideas.

INCREASING EFFICIENCY THROUGH
THE TRANSFER OF BEST PRACTICES

Deborah Copeland, head of BP's business unit for retail operations in the southeastern United States, was looking for ways to improve the performance of her region's BP and Amoco service stations. Through her peer group, she learned of pilot programs at BP stations in the United Kingdom and the Netherlands that were testing some innovative ways to order and deliver convenience store supplies. So last summer, she sought a peer assist from her counterparts in those two countries, as well as from BP retail executives in seven other countries. They met and recommended best practices in such areas as supplier management and store layouts. Copeland then launched three pilot programs at several stores in the Atlanta area. The results, she says, were dramatic. The pilot stores stocked 26% fewer stock-keeping units (or SKUs) than similar control sites; this inventory reduction led to a 20% decrease in working capital even while sales rose 10%. Copeland is currently rolling out the practices across another 62 sites in Atlanta and Orlando, Florida.

IMPROVING THE QUALITY OF DECISIONS
THROUGH PEER ADVICE

When Anne Drinkwater became head of the business unit responsible for transporting Alaska oil from the North Slope to refineries in the western United States, via pipeline and tankers, she didn't know much about shipping. Her previous job had been in the Gulf of Mexico overseeing deepwater oil wells. But a key task after she arrived in Alaska was to decide the number and sizes of tankers her unit needed to handle oil production output over the next 20 years. In addition to enlisting a few experts from the corporate center in England, her project team identified six people from other business units who could help with the decision. In a number of face-to-face and virtual meetings last summer, the group covered issues ranging from long-term oil production forecasts to financing options for the new ships. The final recommendation: buy three new tankers and take options on another three. "In a very supportive way, they challenged some of our thinking and pointed us in the right direction," says Drinkwater, who recently left Alaska to head a BP unit in Norway.

GROWING REVENUE THROUGH SHARED EXPERTISE

In the late 1990s, Graham Hunt was the leader of a BP petrochemical business unit responsible for the design and construction of a $200 million acetic acid plant in western China, to be run as a joint venture with Sinopec, the Chinese petrochemical company. The complexity of bringing such a plant online in so remote a location made it a relatively risky undertaking, so Hunt sought BP expertise from a number of operating units around the world. Over a 30-month period, about 75 people flew to the site in China from different parts of BP for visits lasting from a day to several weeks. They gave advice on technical, legal, tax, safety, accounting, and financial issues. Largely because of this peer assistance, Hunt says, the two-year construction project came in on time and under budget. Production began in November 1998, and the business broke even after only several months of operation. Says Hunt, now chairman of BP China: "We needed expertise and, given our organization, it was often a phone call away."

DEVELOPING NEW BUSINESS OPPORTUNITIES THROUGH THE CROSS-POLLINATION OF IDEAS

Vast but often far-flung pools of ideas and expertise are one of the greatest competitive advantages a large company has in today's knowledge economy. Fruitfully combining this knowledge can produce what might be called "epiphanies of scale"—creative insights that a hot start-up company that has fewer intellectual resources may not be able to achieve. In the spring of 1999, John Melo, then BP's director of brand development, helped oversee an initiative to develop new e-businesses using existing BP assets. In typical BP fashion, managers from some 15 business units met to brainstorm. The effort produced nearly 600 ideas, out of which 150 are currently being developed. For example, BP is working on Flight-needs.com, which will help operators of small to mid-sized jets plan their trips and fueling needs, then furnish fuel at the planned stops. Melo says that the managers from different units "could look at our existing business through a variety of lenses and thus identify hidden opportunities."

MAKING BOLD STRATEGIC MOVES THROUGH THE PROMISE OF WELL-COORDINATED IMPLEMENTATION

David Eyton, currently head of a gas business unit in Trinidad, wasn't alone in wondering how long a massive integration of companies the size of BP and Amoco would take. "It seemed possible that the two companies and cultures could continue to exist indefinitely as parallel universes," he says. But Eyton's peer group at the time—comprising 12 business units, roughly half of them legacy Amoco units—immediately embraced the integration process. Working within the well-established peer group norm of a freewheeling and candid exchange of ideas, the group resolved the staffing issues in two months. One month later, other basic elements of the combined business were put in place. BP executives say it was such flexible peer group behavior that permitted a nearly complete integration of the companies within just 90 days. And that experience helped give BP the confidence to launch another major merger, this time with ARCO, only months later.

Designing the Right Organization: Promote and Discipline

Senior executives who are eager to create new value through a T-shaped management environment must, like the T-shaped managers themselves, find ways to manage some inherent tension in the concept. BP has done that through the combination of *promoting* and *disciplining* horizontal management behavior. Top executives can promote this behavior in several ways without creating an ossifying layer of bureaucracy.

CREATE CLEAR INCENTIVES

Business unit managers at BP are judged on their ability to meet specific performance targets for their units. But they also are rewarded and promoted according to how effectively they—and their staffs—share knowledge with others outside their units. Such behavior "is a key test of a manager's performance and potential," says Nick Butler, the main policy adviser to CEO Browne. "Lone stars"—those who deliver outstanding business unit performance but engage in little cross-unit collaboration—can survive within BP, but their careers typically plateau.

Knowledge-sharing contributions are by their nature more difficult to measure than success at meeting specific unit performance targets. But executives throughout the company say that bosses are generally well aware of the level of their subordinates' cross-unit contributions. And the policy of promoting T-shaped behavior is reinforced by BP's corporate culture. David Nagel recalls his exposure to this shortly after the Amoco merger: "Early on, people on the BP side made it quite clear [to legacy Amoco managers] that you might have spectacular individual business unit performance, but if you weren't seen to be making contributions beyond your own unit, you wouldn't be viewed favorably."

DEVELOP ECONOMIC TRANSPARENCY

Good T-shaped managers don't just provide assistance across business unit boundaries; they also seek help themselves. And one way to encourage such requests is through corporatewide internal-benchmarking systems, which spur managers of underperforming units to ask for help.

When in 1999 Jeanne Johns took over as business unit leader for BP's $1.5 billion oil refinery in Toledo, Ohio, she checked a company database that lists numerous performance and cost metrics for BP's 19 refineries around the world. Some items, such as salaries, clearly were not comparable because of differing business environments. Still, she found that the Toledo facility was lagging far behind its counterparts on a key performance metric—something called "cents per equivalent distillation capacity," which compares the cost of running refineries of different sizes and complexity. The best-performing facility boasted an index of 9 cents per EDC; the Toledo refinery was at 14 cents.

At Johns's request, a team that included some key people from the top-performing refinery, located in Texas, spent a week in Toledo helping her staff identify possible operating improvements. As a result, within nine months, the Toledo refinery reduced its costs to 11 cents per EDC, saving $24 million a year.

FORMALIZE CROSS-UNIT INTERACTIONS

Institutionalizing cross-unit behavior can help sustain something that might otherwise remain ad hoc. The difficulty is to avoid creating the very bureaucracy that working across units is meant to cut through. With its peer groups, BP has tried to achieve this balance. One key, managers say, is the prohibition against managers' superiors participating in peer group meetings, which leads to the mixture of robust confrontation and collegial support that characterizes such gatherings.

David Eyton was the business unit leader of the Wytch Farm oil field in southern England at a time, in the late 1990s, when oil production was beginning to decline in this mature field. Eyton presented to his peer group a 1999 operating budget, excluding onetime items, of $30 million—the same amount as the previous year, even though production was falling. But the

11 other members of the group, in a challenge to the long-standing assumption that unit costs rise as oil production falls in such mature fields, declined to support the proposal. They pushed Eyton to reduce ongoing costs by 20% to keep unit costs flat. "I was shocked," he says. "I had absolutely no idea how to do what they were asking me to do."

Over the next several days of meetings, two members of the group met with him privately and offered not only support but also tips on how to pull this off. After the peer group meeting, Eyton passed the challenge on to his own team. They formed a task force, which visited other business units, including the ones whose leaders had offered the initial challenge. Through such measures as canceling leases on buildings and renegotiating service contracts, Eyton's unit cut its operating costs to $24 million in 1999. More important, his team devised a long-term plan to ensure that operating costs declined in parallel with production for the remainder of the field's life.

Eyton's peer group experience may serve as a convincing example of the benefits of cross-unit behavior. But BP has learned that encouraging such behavior is only half the equation. Senior executives must also monitor and occasionally rein it in. They can discourage ineffective networking in at least two ways:

CURB CROSS-UNIT INTERACTIONS

T-shaped managers need to know that it is not only acceptable but also sometimes wise to refuse requests from other units for their time or the time of their staff. "I could easily wake up every day and find virtually my entire leadership team off at a meeting somewhere around the globe," says Deborah Copeland, the retail unit executive. "While each one of those meetings would benefit the company in some way, there would be hardly anybody left in the office to keep my own business running. In addition, you risk burning your people out with all of this collaboration."

BP executives even talk of occasional outbreaks of "peer assist mania." This is when managers request too many assists, either because they have become swept up with excitement over the potential benefits or, more cynically, because they think peer assists are a key to earning legitimacy within the company. In either case, the excessive requests waste precious time and effort and can undermine faith in the process. Anne Drinkwater, the former business unit leader in Alaska, recalls receiving an invitation to participate in a peer assist gathering that it was clear she could not contribute much to. In fact, she felt the request amounted to no more than an attempt by the requesting manager to check off a box on his annual list of professional objectives. She declined. "You only have so much time," she says, "and you have to prioritize around the right things."

Managers also emphasize that knowledge-sharing activities should focus on business results rather than social events. While social gatherings, like company conferences and off-sites, do help create some comfort level, they also leave managers frustrated because the meetings don't really achieve any business goals. Solving problems together through a results-oriented approach to knowledge sharing is a more potent way to create trust among people from different business units because achieving results together creates a track record showing that people are really helping one another. Trust is a byproduct of effective collaboration.

REPLACE BLOATED ROLODEXES WITH HUMAN PORTALS

Another potential danger for companies seeking the benefits of cross-unit collaboration is overnetworking, with every manager flipping through a bulging Rolodex whenever an issue arises. This is a particularly inefficient way to share expertise: if 100 people want to keep in touch with one another directly, they would need to maintain 4,950 direct relationships—a challenge for even the most ambitious group of T-shaped managers.[4]

Senior executives can minimize this problem by identifying and cultivating a particular type of T-shaped manager, one who connects people seeking information with those who can help them—effectively serving as human portals in the companywide knowledge web. Given the implicit nature of the advice that's typically called for, human portals can't simply reroute information like a switchboard. Rather, they must use their extensive knowledge about who knows what and their understanding of what actually is needed to creatively make connections between information seekers and information holders.

Although business unit heads may be outstanding human portals, often these people connectors can be found further down in the organization. Take Les Owen, an engineer responsible for pipeline technical and regulatory matters in the Alaska business unit that was headed by Anne Drinkwater. "Les is better than a Web site," she says. "He's always helping other people connect. He knows everyone and everything that's going on." Like others at BP who serve this function, Owen carries out his human portal responsibilities as a sidelight to his primary job. Drinkwater had informally ensured that he had time for this role. "I was careful when we agreed on work allocation that I didn't fill 100% of his time," she says.

On average, Owen says, he fields maybe ten phone calls and as many e-mails a week from people outside his business unit trying to locate someone who can help with a problem. Owen, who built up his network of contacts over 26 years at BP in a variety of jobs and locations, says his role goes beyond the company's electronic directory of experts. "Using a database is like picking a name out of a phone book—you don't know the person," he says. "To get an answer they'll have confidence in, people would rather go to contacts they know." (See the exhibit "Human Portals at Work.")

Human Portals at Work

BP cultivates what we call "human portals," a particular type of T-shaped manager who helps people identify third parties in the organization that can provide needed information. Les Owen, a BP engineer in Alaska, is such a manager; like those of his counterparts across the company, his role is informal and in addition to his regular business unit responsibilities. Recently, Owen put a BP engineer seeking information about protecting pipeline facilities from lightning strikes in touch with two engineers elsewhere in the company who were able to help. The exchange—reproduced here in an edited version in which names, locations, and commercially sensitive facts have been changed—is noteworthy not because of its extraordinary results but rather because it's typical of the way Owen and many people like him throughout BP regularly serve as information matchmakers.

From: Larry Watson
To: Les Owen
Subject: Lightning Protection   ①

We haven't talked in a while. Do you know anyone well versed in lightning protection equipment and practices? We've had a lot of problems recently with lightning strikes damaging our pumping facilities.

From: Les Owen
To: Ian French
Subject: RE Lightning Protection   ②

How are things in Houston? I thought you might be able to help with the attached request for information, given your past experience in Larry's part of the world and with lightning-related problems

From: Ian French
To: Nigel Wallace
cc: Les Owen
Subject: RE Lightning Protection   ③

Les Owen, who works for BP Pipelines in Alaska, has been asked by Larry Watson, an engineer at the pipeline unit in Siberia, about recommended practices for lightning protection. Before I follow up, could you respond with any thoughts? They're likely to be particularly interested in equipment and the associated electronics needed for protecting pipeline pumping facilities.

From: Nigel Wallace
To: Ian French
cc: Les Owen
Subject: RE Lightning Protection   ④

There are many claims for exotic lightning protection systems. I prefer to approach the issue with good earthing and earth-bonding practice and the protection of particularly vulnerable components with surge diverter devices. I attach a copy of some useful presentation slides from the BP Electric Network forum in Windsor in November. Call if questions. I'm always happy to provide help in the area of lightning protection—often seen as a black art, though it shouldn't be!

From: Les Owen
To: Larry Watson
Subject: RE Lightning Protection   ⑤

Received the following reply on lightning. I suggest you contact Nigel and Ian directly, who are both in Houston, if you have questions.

A Behavioral Overlay

BP's T-shaped management system isn't the only way a company can share its intellectual resources across business units. One traditional alternative is to centralize knowledge management and decision making, which can be done in a number of ways. The top management team can amass a large number of experts at corporate headquarters. The team can order business unit heads to collaborate. Or it can even combine two or more business units to coordinate their operations and reap the benefits that come from sharing intellectual resources.

While centralizing creates certain economies of both scale and scope, it has a number of serious drawbacks. Centralized knowledge management often breeds a knowledge bureaucracy that is slow to respond to requests for information from managers in the field. It also may fail to capture the latest expertise and ideas from the operating units, where on-the-job learning is constantly evolving. And centralized decision making about knowledge management undermines the benefits of an otherwise decentralized organization, hindering the innovation that can well up when autonomous business units are free to experiment.

By contrast, what BP's T-shaped management approach does, at its core, is to overlay a flexible "behavioral net" onto a decentralized organization structure. Mechanisms such as peer groups, peer assists, dual promotion criteria, and human portals are designed to change managers' daily activities rather than the organizational structure in which they work. And herein lies the key insight from BP's experience. With its behavioral overlay on a decentralized structure, the company can realize the benefits of cross-unit learning and collaboration without having to institute top-down approaches that could undermine the freedom and accountability needed to produce outstanding individual unit performance.

Of course, BP does centralize many decisions and activities, including the design and oversight of information systems and much of its procurement. It even centralizes some specialized technical expertise that is too narrow to be carried by any single business unit. But cross-unit learning is mainly a decentralized and dispersed activity that is based on managers' willingness to work across organizational boundaries.

BP's approach reflects a subtle but vital shift in the sources of advantage for large global companies. In the past, the key advantage large companies had was their ability to pool volume across business units and countries to lower purchasing, component, and production costs and better leverage their brand. These economies are still important, but the benefits of cross-unit learning and collaboration have become much more important in many increasingly knowledge-intensive industries. And while pooling purchasing volumes to get better supplier rates is often best handled by a central purchasing department, the benefits of cross-unit learning tend to be best achieved through decentralized and horizontal networking—that is, directly among employees in operating units who are able to learn, teach, and collaborate.

Companies on the Road to T-Shaped Management

OUR CLOSE EXAMINATION OF BP grew out of a study we conducted of a group of large, global companies that seemed likely to have effective practices for sharing knowledge across units. We conducted interviews with executives at 30 companies, about one-third of them located in Asia, one-third in Europe, and one-third in the United States. The companies represented a wide array of industries, including computers, biotechnology, paper, steel, pharmaceuticals, consumer goods, banking, and high technology.

Although we had, through media searches and discussions with our colleagues, identified in advance those companies that emphasized cross-unit links, we found that few actually benefited broadly from cross-unit learning and collaboration. Many had tried to implement linking mechanisms; they just didn't work very well. For example, several executives described attending frequent off-sites, informational meetings, and conferences convened in the belief that such gatherings would result in greater cooperation and knowledge sharing across units. The problem was that these, on their own, weren't effective. In the words of one manager, "we meet to agree to disagree and schedule another meeting."

In fact, only BP regularly realized the full array of value-creation possibilities we identified in our research. But a handful of companies have had some success collaborating across business and country boundaries.

GlaxoSmithKline

The pharmaceutical company has benefited by encouraging the cross-pollination of ideas through information matchmakers, which we call "human portals." One day, for example, V. Thyagirajan, an area director located in Singapore, received a phone call from Glaxo's managing director in the Philippines, who was looking for new products formulated for his local market. Thyagirajan set up a meeting with the Glaxo managing director in Mumbai, India, someone Thyagirajan knew was also interested in local product development. In a visit to an R&D lab outside Mumbai, the Philippines executive saw that the Indian product developers were working on line extensions of existing antituberculosis medication, a family of drugs not emphasized at the corporate level of the UK-based company. The lab visit sparked a joint effort between the teams in India and the Philippines, and a Philippine researcher moved to the Mumbai facility to help develop new products. The team first came up with a modified anti-TB medication formulated specifically for the Philippines and has subsequently developed other products for the Philippine market.

Siemens

Three years ago, the large German industrial company launched a training program that brings high-potential managers from different divisions together in small teams to solve a problem facing one of the business units. So far, more than 100 teams have been formed. Team members work together for about a year, which includes attending several weeklong meetings at an off-site corporate campus. They then make recommendations to the business unit manager involved, who serves as the team coach during the project. Through the program, team members develop their business skills, build informal relationships across business units, and save the company money—more than $10 million so far—by solving real business problems.

Ispat International

Senior executives at this London-based global steel maker have institutionalized several simple mechanisms for sharing knowledge across their far-flung units that could easily be implemented in companies from many other industries. One is Ispat's policy of cross-directorships, which requires the general manager of every operating unit to sit on the board of at least one other unit. The managing directors of Germany and Trinidad, for instance, sit on each other's boards because they both produce "long" steel products, such as rods and other structural materials. This peer oversight encourages units to adopt best practices from other units—for instance, Germany's successful downsizing initiative. Managing directors of each operating unit also join together every week for a phone meeting that lasts no longer than two hours. Managers report exceptions, nonroutine activities, and things that, in company parlance, "keep them awake at night." In one recent call, the managing director in Trinidad mentioned problems he was having with a transformer that repeatedly failed. As it turned out, managers in Mexico and Canada had similar transformers and were having similar problems. The three units ended up cooperating on both troubleshooting and buying the expertise to perform repairs.

Notes

1. See "What's Your Strategy for Managing Knowledge?" by Morten T. Hansen, Nitin Nohria, and Thomas Tierney, *Harvard Business Review* (March–April 1999).

2. See "Unleashing the Power of Learning: An Interview with British Petroleum's John Browne," by Steven E. Prokesch, *Harvard Business Review* (September–October 1997).

3. We use the term "T-shaped" to refer to a manager's behavior, in contrast to prior uses of the term, where it has typically referred to a manager's skill base. See, for example, the discussion of "T-shaped consultants" in "McKinsey & Company: Managing Knowledge and Learning," by Christopher A. Bartlett, Harvard Business School Case 9-396-357 (1996).

4. The number of connections needed for everybody in an organization to know everybody else is represented by the equation $n(n-1)/2$, where n is the number of people in the organization.

Originally published in March 2001
Reprint R0103G

The Tools of Cooperation and Change

CLAYTON M. CHRISTENSEN, MATT MARX,
AND HOWARD H. STEVENSON

Executive Summary

EMPLOYERS CAN CHOOSE from lots of tools
when they want to encourage employees to work
together toward a new corporate goal. One of the
rarest managerial skills is the ability to understand
which tools will work in a given situation and
which will misfire.

Cooperation tools fall into four major categories:
power, management, leadership, and culture.
Choosing the right tool, say the authors, requires
assessing the organization along two critical
dimensions: the extent to which people agree on
what they want and the extent to which they agree
on *cause and effect*, or how to get what they want.
The authors plot on a matrix where various organizations fall along these two dimensions. Employees

represented in the lower-left quadrant of the model, for example, disagree strongly both about what they want and on what actions will produce which results. Those in the upper-right quadrant agree on both dimensions.

Different quadrants call for different tools. When employees share little consensus on either dimension, for instance, the only methods that will elicit cooperation are "power tools" such as fiat, force, and threats. Yugoslavia's Josip Broz Tito wielded such devices effectively. So did Jamie Dimon, current CEO of JPMorgan Chase, during the bank's integration with Bank One. For employees who agree on what they want but not on how to get it–think of Microsoft in 1995–leadership tools, such as vision statements, are more appropriate.

Some leaders are blessed with an instinct for choosing the right tools–Continental Airlines' Gordon Bethune, General Electric's Jack Welch, and IBM's Lou Gerstner are all examples. Others can use this framework to help select the most appropriate tools for their circumstances.

THE PRIMARY TASK of MANAGEMENT is to get people to work together in a systematic way. Like orchestra conductors, managers direct the talents and actions of various players to produce a desired result. It's a complicated job, and it becomes much more so when managers are trying to get people to change, rather than continue with the status quo. Even the best CEOs can stumble in their attempts to encourage people to work together toward a new corporate goal.

In 1999, for example, Procter & Gamble's Durk Jager, a highly regarded insider who had recently been promoted to CEO, announced Organization 2005, a restructuring program that promised to change P&G's culture. However, not everyone at P&G agreed that such sweeping change was necessary or that the way to achieve it was to reduce investments in the company's core brands in order to fund radical, new products. The organization rebelled, and Jager was forced to resign only 17 months after taking the helm.

The root cause of Jager's very public failure was that he didn't induce P&G employees to cooperate—a requirement of all change campaigns. To achieve such cooperation, managers have a wide variety of tools at their disposal, such as financial incentives, motivational speeches, training programs, and outright threats. But although most competent managers have a good grasp of what cooperation tools are available, we've observed that they may be less sure about which to use. The effectiveness of a given tool depends on the organization's situation. In this article, which employs some ideas from *Do Lunch or Be Lunch,* by Howard Stevenson and Jeffrey Cruikshank, we explain how to choose the right tools and offer advice for managers contemplating change.

Assessing the Existing Level of Agreement

Over our many years observing management successes and failures up close, we've found that the first step in any change initiative must be to assess the level of agreement in the organization along two critical dimensions. The first is the extent to which people agree on *what they want:* the results they seek from their participation in the enterprise; their values and priorities; and which trade-offs they are willing to make in order to achieve those results. Employees at Microsoft, for instance, have historically been united around a common goal: to dominate the desktop. While of course there will always be pockets of employees who are an exception, this theme has defined the company's culture. The second dimension is the extent to which people agree on *cause and effect:* which actions will lead to the desired outcome. When people have a shared understanding of cause and effect, they will probably agree about which processes to adopt—an alignment that was clearly absent at P&G as Jager attempted to transform the company.

The exhibit "The Agreement Matrix" depicts these dimensions. The vertical axis shows agreement by an organization's members on what they want; the horizontal axis shows their agreement on cause and effect. Employees in organizations in the upper-left quadrant share hopes for what they will gain from being part of the organization, even though each might have a different view of what actions will be required to fulfill those hopes. Microsoft found itself in this situation in 1995, when Netscape was threatening to become the primary "window" through which people would use their computers. Everyone in the company wanted the same thing—to preserve Microsoft's domination of the desktop—but initially there was little consensus about how to do that.

Many companies that employ independent contractors and unionized workers, in contrast, are in the lower-right corner. These employees may have little passion for the goals of the company but are willing to follow prescribed procedures if they agree that those actions will produce the needed results.

In the upper-right quadrant are companies whose employees agree on what they want *and* how to get there. Clear consensus on both dimensions makes these organizations' cultures highly resistant to change: People are generally satisfied with what they get out of working in the organization and agree strongly about how to maintain that status quo.

The final scenario is the lower-left quadrant of the agreement matrix, where participants do not agree either on what they want or on how the world works.

The Agreement Matrix

Leaders who want to move their organizations in a new direction must first understand the degree to which employees agree on two dimensions: what they want out of working at the company and cause and effect, or how to achieve what they want. A high level of agreement on both dimensions, such as exists at Apple Computer, requires a completely different set of change tools than leaders will need in, for instance, low-agreement environments.

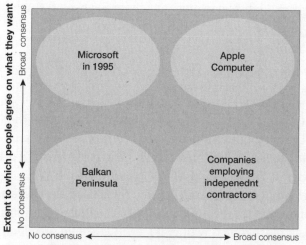

The perpetually warring nation-states of the Balkan Peninsula exemplify this lack of agreement. We will return to each situation in the following pages.

It's important to note that there is no "best" position for managers to aspire to in the agreement matrix. To choose the right tools for fostering cooperation among employees, however, managers must assess where their organization lies. The tools that will induce employees in one quadrant to cooperate with a change program may well misfire with employees in a different quadrant. In fact, in any given situation, most tools for eliciting cooperation will not work.

Moving from Agreement to Cooperation

The tools of cooperation can be grouped into four major categories: power, management, leadership, and culture. In the exhibit "The Four Types of Cooperation Tools," we've matched each category with a quadrant of the agreement matrix. While the boundaries are not rigid, the broad labels can give managers a sense of which tools are likely to be effective in various situations.

POWER TOOLS

When members of an organization share little consensus on either dimension of agreement, the only tools that will elicit cooperation are "power tools" such as fiat, force, coercion, and threats. Marshal Josip Broz Tito, the leader of Yugoslavia during most of the Cold War, wielded power tools effectively. He herded the disparate and antagonistic ethnic groups of the Balkan Peninsula into a more or less artificial nation and said, in effect, "I don't care whether you agree with me or with one

The Four Types of Cooperation Tools

When people in an organization disagree on what they want and on how to achieve desired results, the only tools that induce cooperation are "power tools," which are essentially variations on coercion and fiat. If people want the same thing but disagree on how to achieve it, "leadership tools" such as role modeling and charisma can move them toward a consensus. If people agree strongly on cause and effect but little on what they want, leaders can employ "management tools" such as training and measurement systems. Companies where employees agree on both dimensions of the matrix, and so are generally happy with the status quo, have very strong cultures that are difficult to change. In such circumstances, it is possible only to tweak direction, using such "culture tools" as rituals and folklore. Managers do have other tools at their disposal—such as negotiation and financial incentives—but these will work only when there is a certain level of agreement on both dimensions of the matrix.

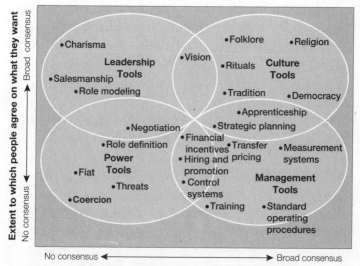

another about what you want out of life or about how to get it. What I want is for you to look down this gun barrel and cooperate." His approach worked, and the Balkan nations lived in relative peace for several decades.

This is not to suggest, of course, that managers bring firearms to the office. But when organizational factions can't agree on what they want or what to do, power tools are the only ones that work. Jamie Dimon, currently the CEO of JPMorgan Chase, used these tools during the bank's integration with his previous company, Bank One. Convinced that pay had gotten out of control (the head of HR at Bank One was paid more than $5 million), Dimon met with executives individually to tell them they were vastly overpaid and slashed hundreds of salaries by 20% to 50%. He drove a replacement of the firm's myriad IT systems with a single platform, threatening to make all the decisions himself if the IT staff didn't reach any decisions in six weeks. He yanked hundreds of unvisited small-to-midsize businesses from the investment bank's "prospects" list so that the commercial bank could have the chance to work with them. Dimon also reconfigured control systems so that retail branch managers, who had received modest bonuses for meeting sales quotas on mortgages and other products, now stood to lose their jobs for missing quotas.

We have included three tools in the exhibit—negotiation, strategic planning, and financial incentives—to make a point. These tools will work only when there is a modicum of agreement on both dimensions of the matrix. In environments of antagonistic disagreement— whether in the Middle East or in the infamous clashes between Eastern Air Lines' management and its machinist union—negotiation generally doesn't work. A leader might use strategic planning to figure out where the organization ought to go next, but in the absence of the requisite degree of agreement on both dimensions, the strategic plan itself won't elicit the cooperative behavior required to get there.

And using financial incentives—essentially paying employees to want what management wants—may backfire in an environment of low consensus. Consider, for example, the world of K-12 public education, which is decidedly in the lower-left quadrant of the agreement matrix. Teachers, taxpayers, administrators, parents, students, and politicians have divergent priorities and disagree strongly about how to improve. Most pay-for-performance schemes have failed miserably in producing enduring change in schools, because financial incentives are a tool that just won't work in this situation.

Power tools can be extremely effective in low-agreement situations. The key is having the authority to use them. Managers sometimes find themselves in balkanized circumstances without the power to wield the only tools that will induce cooperation under those conditions. If managers are asked to lead a matrixed or "lightweight" project team whose members' loyalties are in conflict with the objectives of the project, for instance, the road to success will be tortuous. Just as a carpenter would never undertake a job without having the requisite tools in his or her toolbox, a wise manager in a low-consensus environment would not agree to lead a change program without the authority to wield the right power tools.

MANAGEMENT TOOLS

The tools of cooperation that drive change in the lower-right quadrant of the agreement matrix focus on coordination and processes. These "management tools" include training, standard operating procedures, and measurement systems. For such tools to work, group members need to agree on cause and effect but not necessarily on what they want from their participation in the organization.

For example, in many companies the reasons unionized manufacturing workers come to work are very different from the reasons senior marketing managers do. But if both groups agree that certain manufacturing procedures will result in products with targeted levels of quality and cost, they will cooperate to follow those procedures.

Measurement systems can also elicit cooperation in such situations. During Intel's first two decades, gross-margin-per-wafer-start was the widely agreed-upon metric for profitability. In the 1980s, the company's DRAM products, which had enjoyed high gross margins in the 1970s, were withering under Japanese competition. Focused on the accepted metric—and even without an explicit executive mandate—middle managers in disparate parts of the organization cooperated to shift manufacturing emphasis from DRAMs to microprocessors, which had become higher-margin products.

LEADERSHIP TOOLS

The tools useful in the upper-left quadrant of the agreement matrix tend to be results oriented rather than process oriented. Such "leadership tools" can elicit cooperation as long as there is a high level of consensus that a change is consistent with the reason employees have chosen to work in the enterprise—even if consensus is low on how to achieve the change. Charismatic leaders respected by employees, for example, often do not address how to get things done. Instead, they motivate people to "just go out and do it." Good sales managers employ these tools skillfully.

Bill Gates used the leadership tool we call vision in his 1995 Internet Tidal Wave memo, which helped Microsoft's employees see that maintaining the company's dominance in the software industry (what they wanted) required an aggressive acknowledgment that the nascent World Wide Web would become an integral part of computing rather than a sideshow to the then-dominant desktop applications—an acknowledgment that ran counter to most employees' deeply held beliefs. The fierce response of the company's Internet Explorer team crippled Netscape and won Microsoft a more than 90% share of the browser market. Faced with stiff competition from Google in late 2005, Gates reemployed this technique in his memo regarding a "services wave," calling for a shift from sales of shrink-wrapped software to sales of subscriptions.

The same actions viewed as inspiring and visionary among employees in the upper-left corner of the matrix can be regarded with indifference or disdain by those in the lower quadrants. Consider vision statements. When members of a group agree on what they want to achieve, statements that articulate where the organization needs to go can be energizing and inspiring. But if employees don't agree about what they want, vision statements won't help much in changing their behavior—aside from inducing a collective rolling of eyes.

CULTURE TOOLS

In organizations located in the upper-right quadrant of the matrix, employees will cooperate almost automatically to continue in the same direction. Their deep consensus on priorities, and on what set of actions will allow the company to achieve those priorities, is the essence of a strong culture. As MIT's Edgar Schein wrote in *Organizational Culture and Leadership,* culture is "a pattern of shared basic assumptions that was learned by a group as it solved its problems of external adaptation and internal integration, that has worked well enough to be considered valid and, therefore, to be taught to new members as the correct way to perceive, think, and feel in relation to those problems." In organizations with strong cultures, people instinctively prioritize similar options, and their common view of how the world works means that little debate is necessary about the best way to achieve those priorities. Companies with strong cultures in many ways can be self-managing.

But this very strength can make such organizations highly resistant to change. So-called culture tools—such as rituals and folklore—only facilitate cooperation to preserve the status quo; they are not tools of change. Leadership and management tools can also be used in this quadrant to foster cooperation, but only in order to reinforce or enhance the existing culture. A manager of such a company might see herself as a visionary leader wanting to chart a new course for the organization. She may want to use a vision statement as a tool for analyzing and refining the vision in her mind. But as a tool of change? Employees in the upper-right strong-culture quadrant are unlikely to cooperate with any strategy that is at odds with their deeply shared beliefs about what they want and what must be done. Hewlett-Packard's Carly Fiorina learned this the hard way when she tried to challenge the so-called HP Way. Her very public clashes with HP's employees and board led to her ouster in 2005, following the company's controversial merger with Compaq. Essentially, as P&G's Durk Jager needed to recognize, the only tools that can be wielded are those that are effective in the domain *where the employees are*— and in strong cultures, the tools in the upper-right quadrant lead to cooperation in gradual change, at best.

What Managers Can—and Cannot—Do

We noted earlier that there is no "best" position in the matrix of agreement; each quadrant carries its own challenges. A company's position may reflect where it is in its life cycle and is largely determined by how successful it has been. Most organizations start at the left and often at the bottom of the matrix, where the founder's fiats drive much of what gets prioritized and how it gets done. If employees develop effective methods that result in success, consensus will begin to coalesce on the horizontal dimension of agreement—what actions yield the desired results. As the company succeeds, employees who fit with these ways of working, and who want what senior management wants, tend to be promoted. Those who don't tend to leave. Hence, success is the mechanism that builds consensus around what people want and how they can get it. Success shifts the organization toward the upper-right quadrant.

Crisis and failure, in contrast, can destroy that consensus, plunging the organization toward the lower-left quadrant. Employees in crisis are no longer certain or unanimous in their beliefs about what actions are necessary. Managers who are able and willing to use power tools during crises can get employees to cooperate in a remedial course of action, provided those managers know where the organization needs to go and what must be done to get there. Indeed, scholars of organizational change frequently prescribe "creating a crisis" because it forces employees into a situation where they can be compelled to cooperate.

While there is merit to the create-a-crisis strategy, there's a rub to this simple solution: What if the CEO sees the need to change direction while the business is still healthy—when the crisis is in the future, not the present? And what if this healthy company also has an extremely strong culture? That was the situation facing John Sculley, CEO of Apple Computer from 1983 until 1993. Fresh from a triumphant career at PepsiCo, Sculley was an exceptional executive. During his first several years at Apple, the company continued to prosper. By the late 1980s, however, Sculley sensed trouble over the horizon and saw the need to change strategy in three specific ways. First, he saw fledgling low-cost computer makers, such as Dell, menacingly exploring how to make higher-performance computers within their low-cost business models. Sculley declared that Apple needed to move down-market aggressively, reducing its prices by as much as 75% in order to blunt this disruptive attack. Second, before Microsoft introduced its Windows operating system, Sculley urged Apple to open its proprietary product architecture and begin selling its vaunted operating system. Third, he saw that portable, handheld devices would become an important growth market. In retrospect, Sculley saw the future of his industry with remarkable clarity.

But being a visionary leader isn't all it's cracked up to be. When leaders like Sculley conclude that their organization's course must change, they need to consider where the rest of the employees are in the agreement matrix. At Apple, they were decidedly in the upper-right quadrant—some said that Apple put the "cult" in "culture." Sculley tried reorganization, firings, control systems, financial incentives, training, measurement systems, standard procedures, vision statements, salesmanship, strategic planning, and many more tools to elicit cooperation behind the changes he envisioned. But none worked. The Apple employees wouldn't listen.

Sculley gradually lost credibility with his board and employees as tool after tool failed to produce the changes he desired, and he was ousted in 1993. Apple's board then appointed Michael Spindler, head of the company's successful European operations, as CEO. Spindler also found that the only tools of cooperation at his disposal were those that reinforced Apple's culture, and he was dismissed after three years. The board then brought in Gil Amelio, who had turned around the deeply troubled National Semiconductor—expecting that he could do the same at Apple. He couldn't and was gone in 18 months.

Unable to recruit another qualified CEO, Apple's board turned in desperation to ousted Apple founder Steve Jobs as interim CEO. Jobs essentially stopped trying to change the company and instead encouraged the troops to resume designing cool, innovative, high-end products such as the iMac and iPod. Apple now dominates the digital music industry. But if there had been any tools to wield within this strong culture to elicit cooperation behind the new direction Sculley foresaw, Apple might have captured much of the fruit that ultimately fell into the hands of Compaq, Dell, and Microsoft.

The Tool of Disaggregation

All is not lost for managers who see the need to change a successful company before the onset of a crisis. They can

wield the tool of *disaggregation*—the separation of organizations into units. This allows managers at the new
unit to build a different consensus among its employees
regarding what they want and how to get there, while the
prior culture continues to thrive in the original unit.

Disaggregation works by eliminating the need for
cooperation between groups with opposing goals. This is
how Hewlett-Packard succeeded in the disruptive ink-jet
printer business even while its laser-jet printer business
was prospering with a very different profit model. HP
disaggregated the printer business, leaving the laser-jet
unit in Boise, Idaho, and setting up the ink-jet unit in
Vancouver, Washington. Likewise, IBM stayed strong in
computers for many years, whereas all its mainframe and
minicomputer rivals failed, because it used the tool of
disaggregation. When minicomputers began disrupting
mainframes, IBM created a separate business unit in
Rochester, Minnesota, to focus on minicomputers, which
had to be designed, built, and sold within a very different
economic model than mainframes. When personal computers disrupted minicomputers, IBM disaggregated
again, setting up in Boca Raton, Florida, another freestanding unit, which developed a business model tailored to PCs. Had IBM executives tried to convince the
managers and employees of the original computer business to cooperate on a strategy, economic model, and
culture to succeed simultaneously in mainframes, minicomputers, and PCs, the company would have failed.

Mastering the Tools of Cooperation at Continental Airlines

It would be rare, of course, for *all* employees in a
company to be in one place in the agreement matrix at

a given time or across time. While the founding group of senior managers may be in the upper-right quadrant, manufacturing employees may be in the lower-right. Those in sales and creative design might be in the upper-left, sharing an understanding of what is important but unwilling to subject themselves to the sorts of standards and processes that are effective in the lower-right quadrant. Most managers, unfortunately, have a limited tool kit and thus can successfully manage only in certain types of situations. One of the rarest managerial skills is the ability to understand which tools will work in a given situation—and not to waste energy or risk credibility using tools that won't.

Gordon Bethune, CEO of Continental Airlines from 1994 until 2004, was such a manager. Bethune was the airline's tenth CEO in ten years, following a disastrous run including industry worsts in lost baggage, customer complaints, overbooking, and on-time departures. Moreover, Continental had declared bankruptcy twice during the previous decade and was losing $55 million per month despite years of cost cutting.

Bethune turned down the top job twice even though he was already serving as Continental's COO. The first offer was to be acting CEO during the existing CEO's six-month leave of absence, and the second was to serve in the office of the CEO after that executive decided to retire. Although board members respected Bethune, they believed that the only way to restore profitability was through further cost cutting—a path Bethune was convinced would lead to disaster, not deliverance. Given the significant disagreement about how to restore profitability, Bethune knew he could do nothing without the full authority that came with the top job, without the qualifiers of "acting" or "office of."

Even after the board approved Bethune as CEO, few
within the company agreed with his unconventional
view that Continental needed to be *less* restrictive of its
employees and spend *more* in order to get out of bankruptcy. As Bethune wrote in his book *From Worst to
First,* when the operations staff rebuffed his instruction
to repaint all of the carrier's more than 200 airplanes,
he threatened to shoot them unless they complied.
Concerned that customer-service employees were
micromanaging customers by relying too heavily on a
very thick instruction manual, he set fire to a stack of
manuals in the parking lot.

Having won some initial battles by sheer force,
Bethune achieved preliminary success and began to
move the company out of the lower-left quadrant toward
the upper-right. As the company started to recover,
Bethune began employing more traditional management
tools, including financial incentives. After he offered
each employee a $65 bonus every month that Continen-
tal placed among the top five for on-time departures,
Continental jumped to fourth the subsequent month and
first thereafter. Our model suggests that this incentive
would not have worked in the environment of distrust
and disagreement that characterized the company when
Bethune began his work. By 1998, the company had
posted 11 straight quarters of improved profits and had
won two consecutive J.D. Power and Associates' awards.
Bethune spent the final years of his career using the tools
in the upper-right quadrant, working to reinforce what
has become a very productive culture.

Bethune's well-timed choice of tools mirrored that of
Jack Welch at General Electric, who started out as Neu-
tron Jack, using power tools when the company was a
collection of businesses with vastly different cultures,

operating procedures, and expectations about growth and profitability. As he oriented the company around the mantra of being first or second in each of the conglomerate's businesses, GE moved from the lower-left corner of the matrix toward the upper-right, and Welch shifted his focus to culture-reinforcing activities, teaching up-and-coming managers at the company's Crotonville campus.

The success of Bethune and Welch, of course, is both good news and bad news for their successors. As long as the shared purposes and unified view of how to achieve them are appropriate for their companies' challenges, Larry Kellner and Jeffrey Immelt ought to be able to preside over continued success using the cooperation tools handed to them on their arrival. However, if there are shifts in the competitive environment that mandate significant changes either to what people want or to the required actions, the two CEOs may find that the tools their predecessors used to turn their organizations around cannot be wielded effectively in the strong-culture quadrant.

For example, much has been written about former CEO Lou Gerstner's success in refashioning IBM from a "big iron" company to one built on services. Managing change is always hard. But our model suggests that because he took IBM's helm when the company was in genuine crisis, losing billions of dollars, Gerstner was fortunate. The situation demanded power tools. As IBM's service businesses mature, his successor, Sam Palmisano, may face the tougher challenge. There is no current crisis that enables the effective use of power tools to marshal a cooperative march in a new direction. He faces a cultural challenge that will likely prove more difficult than the crisis Gerstner faced.

Bethune, Welch, and Gerstner were blessed with an instinct for choosing the right tools at the right time. Our hope is that by making the instincts of effective managers more explicit, even those of us who are not born knowing how to manage change can learn to do so more effectively.

The Tools of Politics

IN INSTITUTIONS WITH WELL-ESTABLISHED CULTURES (those in the upper-right portion of the exhibit "The Agreement Matrix"), democracy can be used as a tool to encourage cooperation. An important insight from this model is that democracy will not work except where people agree strongly on both dimensions of the matrix: what they want and the rules of cause and effect. The very functioning of democracy depends upon the existence of strong cultural beliefs that are often rooted in the teachings of certain religions. The religious institutions at the root of these cultures have taught that people are meant to be free and that they should voluntarily be honest and respect the life, property, and equal opportunity of others—because even if the police don't catch and punish them, they will be rewarded or punished in some way in the afterlife. The successful practice of these beliefs—together with a shared value that every person should be allowed to worship God in his or her own way—has created successful societies in places such as India, Japan, the United States, and Western Europe. The practices have become so deeply embedded over so many years that almost all people in these societies, regardless of religious belief, now strongly share these values and are ensconced in the upper-right quadrant of the agreement matrix. The vast majority of people living in these cultures obey the law voluntarily—and, as a result, democracy works.

On occasion, Americans in particular have tried to impose democracy on countries whose populations are not in the upper-right corner of the agreement matrix—where religious or other institutions have not built the type of cultural consensus that is consistent with democratic principles. When America has essentially snapped its fingers at these countries, ordering them to establish stable democracies—and quickly—chaos typically has ensued. The crime, corruption, and tax evasion that characterize much of Russia; the collapse of civil order that torments Haiti; and the costly, tragic dilemma that America now faces in Iraq—all are testaments to the fact that democracy doesn't work when the enabling preconditions don't exist.

Originally published in October 2006
Reprint R0610D

Building the *Emotional Intelligence* of Groups

VANESSA URCH DRUSKAT

AND STEVEN B. WOLFF

W HEN MANAGERS FIRST STARTED HEARING
about the concept of emotional intelligence in the 1990s,
scales fell from their eyes. The basic message, that effectiveness in organizations is at least as much about EQ as
IQ, resonated deeply; it was something that people knew
in their guts but that had never before been so well articulated. Most important, the idea held the potential for
positive change. Instead of being stuck with the hand
they'd been dealt, people could take steps to enhance
their emotional intelligence and make themselves more
effective in their work and personal lives.

Indeed, the concept of emotional intelligence had real
impact. The only problem is that so far emotional intelligence has been viewed only as an individual competency,
when the reality is that most work in organizations is
done by teams. And if managers have one pressing need
today, it's to find ways to make teams work better.

It is with real excitement, therefore, that we share these findings from our research: individual emotional intelligence has a group analog, and it is just as critical to groups' effectiveness. Teams can develop greater emotional intelligence and, in so doing, boost their overall performance.

Why Should Teams Build Their Emotional Intelligence?

No one would dispute the importance of making teams work more effectively. But most research about how to do so has focused on identifying the task processes that distinguish the most successful teams—that is, specifying the need for cooperation, participation, commitment to goals, and so forth. The assumption seems to be that, once identified, these processes can simply be imitated by other teams, with similar effect. It's not true. By analogy, think of it this way: a piano student can be taught to play Minuet in G, but he won't become a modern-day Bach without knowing music theory and being able to play with heart. Similarly, the real source of a great team's success lies in the fundamental conditions that allow effective task processes to emerge—and that cause members to engage in them wholeheartedly.

Our research tells us that three conditions are essential to a group's effectiveness: trust among members, a sense of group identity, and a sense of group efficacy. When these conditions are absent, going through the motions of cooperating and participating is still possible. But the team will not be as effective as it could be, because members will choose to hold back rather than fully engage. To be most effective, the team needs to create emotionally intelligent norms—the attitudes and behaviors that eventually become habits—that support behaviors for building trust, group identity, and group efficacy. The outcome is complete engagement in tasks. (For more on how emotional intelligence influences these conditions, see the insert "A Model of Team Effectiveness" at the end of this article.)

Three Levels of Emotional Interaction

Make no mistake: a team with emotionally intelligent members does not necessarily make for an emotionally intelligent group. A team, like any social group, takes on its own character. So creating an upward, self-reinforcing spiral of trust, group identity, and group efficacy requires more than a few members who exhibit emotionally intelligent behavior. It requires a team atmosphere in which the norms build emotional capacity (the ability to respond constructively in emotionally uncomfortable situations) and influence emotions in constructive ways.

Team emotional intelligence is more complicated than individual emotional intelligence because teams interact at more levels. To understand the differences, let's first look at the concept of individual emotional intelligence as defined by Daniel Goleman. In his definitive book *Emotional Intelligence,* Goleman explains the chief characteristics of someone with high EI; he or she is *aware* of emotions and able to *regulate* them—and this awareness and regulation are directed both *inward,* to one's self, and *outward,* to others. "Personal competence," in Goleman's words, comes from being aware of and regulating one's own emotions. "Social competence"is awareness and regulation of others' emotions.

A group, however, must attend to yet another level of awareness and regulation. It must be mindful of the emotions of its members, its own group emotions or moods, and the emotions of other groups and individuals outside its boundaries.

In this article, we'll explore how emotional incompetence at any of these levels can cause dysfunction. We'll also show how establishing specific group norms that create awareness and regulation of emotion at these three levels can lead to better outcomes. First, we'll focus on the individual level—how emotionally intelligent groups work with their individual members' emotions. Next, we'll focus on the group level. And finally, we'll look at the cross-boundary level.

Working with Individuals' Emotions

Jill Kasper, head of her company's customer service department, is naturally tapped to join a new cross-functional team focused on enhancing the customer experience: she has extensive experience in and a real passion for customer service. But her teammates find she brings little more than a bad attitude to the table. At an early brainstorming session, Jill sits silent, arms crossed, rolling her eyes. Whenever the team starts to get energized about an idea, she launches into a detailed account of how a similar idea went nowhere in the past. The group is confused: this is the customer service star they've been hearing about? Little do they realize she feels insulted by the very formation of the team. To her, it implies she hasn't done her job well enough.

When a member is not on the same emotional wavelength as the rest, a team needs to be emotionally intelligent vis-à-vis that individual. In part, that simply means being aware of the problem. Having a norm that encourages interpersonal understanding might facilitate an awareness that Jill is acting out of defensiveness. And picking up on this defensiveness is necessary if the team wants to make her understand its desire to amplify her good work, not negate it.

Some teams seem to be able to do this naturally. At Hewlett-Packard, for instance, we learned of a team that was attempting to cross-train its members. The idea was that if each member could pinch-hit on everyone else's job, the team could deploy efforts to whatever task required the most attention. But one member seemed very uncomfortable with learning new skills and tasks; accustomed to being a top producer in his own job, he hated not knowing how to do a job perfectly. Luckily, his team-mates recognized his discomfort, and rather than being annoyed, they redoubled their efforts to support him. This team benefited from a group norm it had established over time emphasizing interpersonal understanding. The norm had grown out of the group's realization that working to accurately hear and understand one another's feelings and concerns improved member morale and a willingness to cooperate.

Many teams build high emotional intelligence by taking pains to consider matters from an individual member's perspective. Think of a situation where a team of four must reach a decision; three favor one direction and the fourth favors another. In the interest of expedience, many teams in this situation would move directly to a majority vote. But a more emotionally intelligent group would pause first to hear out the objection. It would also ask if everyone were completely behind the decision, even if there appeared to be consensus. Such groups would ask, "Are there any perspectives we haven't heard yet or thought through completely?"

Perspective taking is a team behavior that teamwork experts discuss often—but not in terms of its emotional consequence. Many teams are trained to use perspective-taking techniques to make decisions or solve problems (a common tool is affinity diagramming). But these techniques may or may not improve a group's emotional intelligence. The problem is that many of these techniques consciously attempt to remove emotion from the process by collecting and combining perspectives in a mechanical way. A more effective approach to perspective taking is to ensure that team members see one another making the effort to grapple with perspectives; that way, the team has a better chance of creating the kind of trust that leads to greater participation among members.

An executive team at the Hay Group, a consulting firm, engages in the kind of deep perspective taking we're describing. The team has done role-playing exercises in which members adopt others' opinions and styles of interaction. It has also used a "storyboarding" technique, in which each member creates a small poster representing his or her ideas. As team members will attest, these methods and others have helped the group build trust and increase participation.

Regulating Individuals' Emotions

Interpersonal understanding and perspective taking are two ways that groups can become more aware of their members' perspectives and feelings. But just as important as awareness is the ability to regulate those emotions—to have a positive impact on how they are expressed and even on how individual team members feel. We're not talking about imposing groupthink or some other form of manipulation here—clearly, the goal must be to balance the team's cohesion with members' individuality. We're simply acknowledging that people take their emotional cues from those around them. Something that seems upsetting initially can seem not so bad—or ten times worse—depending on whether one's colleagues are inclined to smooth feathers or fan flames. The most constructive way of regulating team members' emotions is by establishing norms in the group for both confrontation and caring.

It may seem illogical to suggest that an emotionally intelligent group must engage in confrontation, but it's not. Inevitably, a team member will indulge in behavior that crosses the line, and the team must feel comfortable calling the foul. In one manufacturing team we studied, a member told us about the day she selfishly decided to extend her break. Before long, one of her teammates stormed into the break room, saying, "What are you doing in here? Get back out on the floor—your team needs you!" The woman had overstepped the bounds, and she got called on it. There were no hard feelings, because the woman knew the group valued her contributions.

Some teams also find that a little humor helps when pointing out errant behavior. Teasing someone who is habitually late for meetings, for instance, can make that person aware of how important timeliness is to the group. Done right, confrontation can be seen in a positive light; it's a way for the group to say, "We want you in—we need your contribution." And it's especially important when a team must work together on a long-term assignment. Without confrontation, disruptive behavior can fester and erode a sense of trust in a team.

Establishing norms that reinforce caring behavior is often not very difficult and usually a matter of concentrating on little things. When an individual is upset, for example, it may make all the difference to have group members acknowledge that person's feelings. We saw this in a meeting where one team member arrived angry because the time and place of the meeting was very inconvenient for him. When another member announced the sacrifice the man had made to be there, and thanked him, the man's attitude turned around 180 degrees. In general, a caring orientation includes displaying positive regard, appreciation, and respect for group members through behaviors such as support, validation, and compassion.

Interpersonal understanding, perspective taking, confrontation, caring—these norms build trust and a sense of group identity among members. And all of them can be established in teams where they don't arise naturally. You may ask, But is it really worth all the effort? Does it make sense to spend managerial time fostering new norms to accommodate a few prickly personalities? Of course it does. Teams are at the very foundation of an organization, and they won't work effectively without mutual trust and a common commitment to goals.

Working with Group Emotions

Chris couldn't believe it, but he was requesting a reassignment. The team he was on was doing good work, staying on budget, and hitting all its deadlines—though not always elegantly. Its leader, Stan Evans, just got a promotion. So why was being on the team such a downer? At the last major status meeting, they should have been serving champagne—so much had been achieved. Instead, everyone was thoroughly dispirited over a setback they hadn't foreseen, which turned out later to be no big deal. It seemed no matter what happened, the group griped. The team even saw Stan's promotion in a negative light: "Oh, so I guess management wants to keep a closer eye on us" and "I hear Stan's new boss doesn't back this project." Chris had a friend on another team who was happy to put in a good word for him. The work was inherently less interesting—but hey, at least they were having fun.

Some teams suffer because they aren't aware of emotions at the group level. Chris's team, for instance, isn't aware of all it has achieved, and it doesn't acknowledge that it has fallen into a malaise. In our study of effective teams, we've found that having norms for group self-awareness—of emotional states, strengths and weaknesses, modes of interaction, and task processes—is a critical part of group emotional intelligence that facilitates group efficacy. Teams gain it both through self-evaluation and by soliciting feedback from others.

Self-evaluation can take the form of a formal event or a constant activity. At Sherwin Williams, a group of managers was starting a new initiative that would require higher levels of teamwork. Group members hired a consultant, but before the consultant arrived, they met to assess their strengths and weaknesses as a team. They found that merely articulating the issues was an important step toward building their capabilities.

A far less formal method of raising group emotional awareness is through the kind of activity we saw at the Veterans Health Administration's Center for Leadership and Development. Managers there have developed a norm in which they are encouraged to speak up when they feel the group is not being productive. For example, if there's a post-lunch lull and people on the team are low on energy, someone might say, "Don't we look like a bunch of sad sacks?" With attention called to it, the group makes an effort to refocus.

Emotionally competent teams don't wear blinders; they have the emotional capacity to face potentially difficult information and actively seek opinions on their task processes, progress, and performance from the outside. For some teams, feedback may come directly from customers. Others look to colleagues within the company, to suppliers, or to professional peers. A group of designers we studied routinely posts its work in progress on walls throughout the building, with invitations to comment and critique. Similarly, many advertising agencies see annual industry competitions as a valuable source of feedback on their creative teams' work.

Regulating Group Emotions

Many teams make conscious efforts to build team spirit. Team-building outings, whether purely social or Outward Bound–style physical challenges, are popular methods for building this sense of collective enthusiasm. What's going on here is that teams and their leaders recognize they can improve a team's overall attitude—that is, they are regulating group-level emotion. And while the focus of a team-building exercise is often not directly related to a group's actual work, the benefits are highly relevant: teams come away with higher emotional capacity and thus a greater ability to respond to emotional challenges.

The most effective teams we have studied go far beyond the occasional "ropes and rocks" off-site. They have established norms that strengthen their ability to respond effectively to the kind of emotional challenges a group confronts on a daily basis. The norms they favor accomplish three main things: they create resources for working with emotions, foster an affirmative environment, and encourage proactive problem solving.

Teams need resources that all members can draw on to deal with group emotions. One important resource is a common vocabulary. To use an example, a group member at the Veterans Health Administration picked up on another member's bad mood and told him that he was just "cranky" today. The "cranky" term stuck and became the group's gentle way of letting someone know that their negativity was having a bad effect on the group. Other resources may include helpful ways to vent frustrations. One executive team leader we interviewed described his team's practice of making time for a "wailing wall"—a few minutes of whining and moaning about some setback. Releasing and acknowledging those negative emotions, the leader says, allows the group to refocus its attention on the parts of the situation it can control and channel its energy in a positive direction. But sometimes, venting takes more than words. We've seen more than one intense workplace outfitted with toys—like soft projectile shooters—that have been used in games of cube warfare.

Perhaps the most obvious way to build emotional capacity through regulating team-level emotion is simply to create an affirmative environment. Everyone values a team that, when faced with a challenge, responds with a can-do attitude. Again, it's a question of having the right group norms—in this case, favoring optimism, and positive images and interpretations over negative ones. This doesn't always come naturally to a team, as one executive we interviewed at the Hay Group knows. When external conditions create a cycle of negativity among group members, he takes it upon himself to change the atmosphere of the group. He consciously resists the temptation to join the complaining and blaming and instead tries to reverse the cycle with a positive, constructive note.

One of the most powerful norms we have seen for building a group's ability to respond to emotionally challenging situations is an emphasis on proactive problem solving. We saw a lot of this going on in a manufacturing team we observed at AMP Corporation. Much of what this team needed to hit its targets was out of its strict control. But rather than sit back and point fingers, the team worked hard to get what it needed from others, and in some cases, took matters into its own hands. In one instance, an alignment problem in a key machine was creating faulty products. The team studied the problem and approached the engineering group with its own suggested design for a part that might correct the problem. The device worked, and the number of defective products decreased significantly.

This kind of problem solving is valuable for many reasons. It obviously serves the company by removing one more obstacle to profitability. But, to the point of our work, it also shows a team in control of its own emotions. It refused to feel powerless and was eager to take charge.

Working with Emotions Outside the Group

Jim sighed. The "Bugs" team was at it again. Didn't they see that while they were high-fiving one another over their impressive productivity, the rest of the organization was paying for it? This time, in their self-managed wisdom, they'd decided to make a three months' supply of one component. No changeover meant no machine downtime and a record low cost per unit. But now the group downstream was swamped with inventory it didn't need and worried about shortages of something else. Jim braced himself for his visit to the floor. The Bugs didn't take criticism well;

they seemed to think they were flawless and that everyone else was just trying to take them down a notch. And what was with that name, anyway? Some kind of inside joke, Jim guessed. Too bad nobody else got it.

The last kind of emotional intelligence any high-performing team should have relates to cross-boundary relationships. Just as individuals should be mindful of their own emotions and others', groups should look both inward and outward emotionally. In the case of the Bugs, the team is acting like a clique—creating close emotional ties within but ignoring the feelings, needs, and concerns of important individuals and teams in the broader organization.

Some teams have developed norms that are particularly helpful in making them aware of the broader organizational context. One practice is to have various team members act as liaisons to important constituencies. Many teams are already made up of members drawn from different parts of an organization, so a cross-boundary perspective comes naturally. Others need to work a little harder. One team we studied realized it would be important to understand the perspective of its labor union. Consequently, a team member from HR went to some lengths to discover the right channels for having a union member appointed to the group. A cross-boundary perspective is especially important in situations where a team's work will have significant impact on others in the organization—for example, where a team is asked to design an intranet to serve everyone's needs. We've seen many situations in which a team is so enamored of its solution that it is caught completely by surprise when others in the company don't share its enthusiasm.

Some of the most emotionally intelligent teams we have seen are so attuned to their broader organizational context that it affects how they frame and communicate their own needs and accomplishments. A team at the chemical-processing company KoSa, for example, felt it needed a new piece of manufacturing equipment, but senior management wasn't so sure the purchase was a priority. Aware that the decision makers were still on the fence, the team decided to emphasize the employee safety benefits of the new machine—just one aspect of its desirability to them, but an issue of paramount importance to management. At a plant safety meeting attended by high-level managers, they made the case that the equipment they were seeking would greatly reduce the risk of injury to workers. A few weeks later they got it.

Sometimes, a team must be particularly aware of the needs and feelings of another group within the organization. We worked with an information technology company where the hardware engineers worked separately from the software engineers to achieve the same goal—faster processing and fewer crashes. Each could achieve only so much independently. When finally a hardware team leader went out of his way to build relationships with the software people, the two teams began to cooperate—and together, they achieved 20% to 40% higher performance than had been targeted.

This kind of positive outcome can be facilitated by norms that encourage a group to recognize the feelings and needs of other groups. We saw effective norms for interteam awareness at a division of AMP, where each manufacturing team is responsible for a step in the manufacturing process and they need one another to complete the product on time. Team leaders there meet in the morning to understand the needs, resources, and schedules of each team. If one team is ahead and another is behind, they reallocate resources. Members of the faster team help the team that's behind and do so in a friendly way that empathizes with their situation and builds the relationship.

Most of the examples we've been citing show teams that are not only aware of but also able to influence outsiders' needs and perspectives. This ability to regulate emotion at the cross-boundary level is a group's version of the "social skills" so critical to individual emotional intelligence. It involves developing external relationships and gaining the confidence of outsiders, adopting an ambassadorial role instead of an isolationist one.

A manufacturing team we saw at KoSa displayed very high social skills in working with its maintenance team. It recognized that, when problems occurred in the plant, the maintenance team often had many activities on its plate. All things being equal, what would make the maintenance team consider this particular manufacturing group a high priority? Knowing a good relationship would be a factor, the manufacturing team worked hard to build good ties with the maintenance people. At one point, for instance, the manufacturing team showed its appreciation by nominating the maintenance team for "Team of the Quarter" recognition—and then doing all the letter writing and behind-the-scenes praising that would ultimately help the maintenance team win. In turn, the manufacturing team's good relationship with maintenance helped it become one of the highest producers in the plant.

A Model for Group Emotional Intelligence

We've been discussing the need for teams to learn to channel emotion effectively at the three levels of human

interaction important to them: team to individual
member, team to itself, and team to outside entities.
Together, the norms we've been exploring help groups
work with emotions productively and intelligently.
Often, groups with emotionally intelligent members have
norms like these in place, but it's unlikely any group
would unconsciously come up with *all* the norms we
have outlined. In other words, this is a model for group
emotional intelligence that any work team could benefit
from by applying it deliberately.

What would the ultimate emotionally intelligent team
look like? Closest to the ideal are some of the teams
we've seen at IDEO, the celebrated industrial design firm.
IDEO's creative teams are responsible for the look and
feel of products like Apple's first mouse, the Crest tooth-
paste tube, and the Palm V personal digital assistant.
The firm routinely wins competitions for the form and
function of its designs and even has a business that
teaches creative problem-solving techniques to other
companies.

The nature of IDEO's work calls for high group emotional intelligence. Under pressure of client deadlines
and budget estimates, the company must deliver innovative, aesthetic solutions that balance human needs with
engineering realities. It's a deep philosophical belief at
IDEO that great design is best accomplished through the
creative friction of diverse teams and not the solitary
pursuit of brilliant individuals, so it's imperative that the
teams at IDEO click. In our study of those teams, we
found group norms supporting emotional intelligence at
all three levels of our model.

First, the teams at IDEO are very aware of individual
team members' emotions, and they are adept at regulating them. For example, an IDEO designer became very

frustrated because someone from marketing was insisting a logo be applied to the designer's product, which he felt would ruin it visually. At a meeting about the product, the team's project leader picked up on the fact that something was wrong. The designer was sitting off by himself, and things "didn't look right." The project leader looked into the situation and then initiated a negotiation that led to a mutual solution.

IDEO team members also confront one another when they break norms. This is common during brainstorming sessions, where the rule is that people must defer judgment and avoid shooting down ideas. If someone breaks that norm, the team comes down on him in a playful yet forceful way (imagine being pelted by foam toys). Or if someone is out of line, the norm is to stand up and call her on it immediately. If a client is in the room, the confrontation is subtler—perhaps a kick under the chair.

Teams at IDEO also demonstrate strengths in group-focused emotional intelligence. To ensure they have a high level of self-awareness, teams constantly seek feedback from both inside and outside the organization. Most important, they work very closely with customers. If a design is not meeting customer expectations, the team finds out quickly and takes steps to modify it.

Regulating group emotion at IDEO often means providing outlets for stress. This is a company that believes in playing and having fun. Several hundred finger blasters (a toy that shoots soft projectiles) have been placed around the building for employees to pick up and start shooting when they're frustrated. Indeed, the design firm's culture welcomes the expression of emotions, so it's not uncommon for someone—whether happy or angry—to stand up and yell. IDEO has even created fun office projects that people can work on if they need a break. For example, they might have a project to design the company holiday card or to design the "tourist stop" displays seen by visitors.

Finally, IDEO teams also have norms to ensure they are aware of the needs and concerns of people outside their boundaries and that they use that awareness to develop relationships with those individuals and groups. On display at IDEO is a curious model: a toy truck with plastic pieces on springs that pop out of the bed of the truck when a button is pressed. It turns out the model commemorates an incident that taught a variety of lessons. The story centers on a design team that had been working for three weeks on a very complex plastic enclosure for a product. Unfortunately, on the Thursday before a Monday client deadline, when an engineer was taking it to be painted, it slipped from his pickup bed and exploded on the road at 70 mph. The team was willing to work through the weekend to rebuild the part but couldn't finish it without the help of the outside fabricator it had used on the original. Because they had taken the time to build a good relationship with the fabricator, its people were willing to go above and beyond the call of duty. The lighthearted display was a way for teammates to show the engineer that all was forgiven—and a reminder to the rest of the organization of how a team in crisis can get by with a little help from its friends.

Where Do Norms Come From?

Not every company is as dependent on teams and their emotional intelligence as IDEO. But now more than ever, we see companies depending on teams for decisions and tasks that, in another time, would have been the work of individuals. And unfortunately, we also see them discovering that a team can have everything going for it—the brightest and most qualified people, access to resources, a clear mission—but still fail because it lacks group emotional intelligence.

Norms that build trust, group identity, and group efficacy are the key to making teams click. They allow an otherwise highly skilled and resourced team to fulfill its potential, and they can help a team faced with substantial challenges achieve surprising victories. So how do norms as powerful as the ones we've described in this article come about? In our research, we saw them being introduced from any of five basic directions: by formal team leaders, by informal team leaders, by courageous followers, through training, or from the larger organizational culture. (For more on how to establish the norms described in this article, see the insert "Building Norms for Three Levels of Group Emotional Intelligence" at the end of this article.)

At the Hay Group, for example, it was the deliberate action of a team leader that helped one group see the importance of emotions to the group's overall effectiveness. Because this particular group was composed of managers from many different cultures, its leader knew he couldn't assume all the members possessed a high level of interpersonal understanding. To establish that norm, he introduced novelties like having a meeting without a table, using smaller groups, and conducting an inventory of team members' various learning styles.

Interventions like these can probably be done only by a formal team leader. The ways informal leaders or other team members enhance emotional intelligence are typically more subtle, though often just as powerful. Anyone might advance the cause, for example, by speaking up if the group appears to be ignoring an important perspective or feeling—or simply by doing his or her part to create an affirmative environment.

Training courses can also go a long way toward increasing emotional awareness and showing people how to regulate emotions. We know of many companies that now focus on emotional issues in leadership development courses, negotiation and communication workshops, and employee-assistance programs like those for stress management. These training programs can sensitize team members to the importance of establishing emotionally intelligent norms.

Finally, perhaps more than anything, a team can be influenced by a broader organizational culture that recognizes and celebrates employee emotion. This is clearly the case at IDEO and, we believe, at many of the companies creating the greatest value in the new economy. Unfortunately, it's the most difficult piece of the puzzle to put in place at companies that don't already have it. For organizations with long histories of employees checking their emotions at the door, change will occur, if at all, one team at a time.

Becoming Intelligent About Emotion

The research presented in this article arose from one simple imperative: in an era of teamwork, it's essential to figure out what makes teams work. Our research shows that, just like individuals, the most effective teams are emotionally intelligent ones—and that any team can attain emotional intelligence.

In this article, we've attempted to lay out a model for positive change, containing the most important types of norms a group can create to enhance its emotional intelligence. Teams, like all groups, operate according to such norms. By working to establish norms for emotional awareness and regulation at all levels of interaction, teams can build the solid foundation of trust, group identity, and group efficacy they need for true cooperation and collaboration—and high performance overall.

A Model of Team Effectiveness

STUDY AFTER STUDY HAS SHOWN that teams are more creative and productive when they can achieve high levels of participation, cooperation, and collaboration among members. But interactive behaviors like these aren't easy to legislate. Our work shows that three basic conditions need to be present before such behaviors can occur: mutual trust among members, a sense of group identity (a feeling among members that they belong to a unique and worthwhile group), and a sense of group efficacy (the belief that the team can perform well and that group members are more effective working together than apart).

At the heart of these three conditions are emotions. Trust, a sense of identity, and a feeling of efficacy arise in environments where emotion is well handled, so groups stand to benefit by building their emotional intelligence.

Group emotional intelligence isn't a question of dealing with a necessary evil– catching emotions as they bubble up and promptly suppressing them. Far from it. It's about bringing emotions deliberately to the surface and understanding how they affect the team's work. It's also about behaving in ways that build relationships both inside and outside the team and that strengthen the team's ability to face challenges. Emotional intelligence means exploring, embracing, and ultimately relying on emotion in work that is, at the end of the day, deeply human.

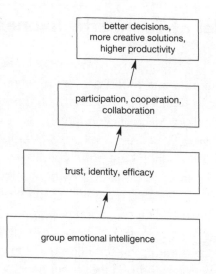

Building Norms for Three Levels of Group Emotional Intelligence

GROUP EMOTIONAL INTELLIGENCE is about the small acts that make a big difference. It is not about a team member working all night to meet a deadline; it is about saying thank you for doing so. It is not about in-depth discussion of ideas; it is about asking a quiet member for his thoughts.

Individual	Group	Cross-Boundary

Norms That Create Awareness of Emotions

Cross-Boundary

Organizational Understanding

1. Find out the concerns and needs of others in the organization.

2. Consider who can influence the team's ability to accomplish its goals.

3. Discuss the culture and politics in the organization.

4. Ask whether proposed team actions are congruent with the organization's culture and politics.

Group

Team Self-Evaluation

1. Schedule time to examine team effectiveness.

2. Create measurable task and process objectives and then measure them.

3. Acknowledge and discuss group moods.

4. Communicate your sense of what is transpiring in the team.

5. Allow members to call a "process check." (For instance, a team member might say, "Process check: is this the most effective use of our time right now?")

Seeking Feedback

1. Ask your "customers" how you are doing.

2. Post your work and invite comments.

3. Benchmark your processes.

Individual

Interpersonal Understanding

1. Take time away from group tasks to get to know one another.

2. Have a "check in" at the beginning of the meeting—that is, ask how everyone is doing.

3. Assume that undesirable behavior takes place for a reason. Find out what that reason is. Ask questions and listen. Avoid negative attributions.

4. Tell your teammates what you're thinking and how you're feeling.

Perspective Taking

1. Ask whether everyone agrees with a decision.

2. Ask quiet members what they think.

3. Question decisions that come too quickly.

4. Appoint a devil's advocate.

Norms That Help Regulate Emotions

Confronting

1. Set ground rules and use them to point out errant behavior.
2. Call members on errant behavior.
3. Create playful devices for pointing out such behavior. These often emerge from the group spontaneously. Reinforce them.

Caring

1. Support members: volunteer to help them if they need it; be flexible, and provide emotional support.
2. Validate members' contributions. Let members know they are valued.
3. Protect members from attack.
4. Respect individuality and differences in perspectives. Listen.
5. Never be derogatory or demeaning.

Creating Resources for Working with Emotion

1. Make time to discuss difficult issues, and address the emotions that surround them.
2. Find creative, shorthand ways to acknowledge and express the emotion in the group.
3. Create fun ways to acknowledge and relieve stress and tension.
4. Express acceptance of members' emotions.

Creating an Affirmative Environment

1. Reinforce that the team can meet a challenge. Be optimistic. For example, say things like, "We can get through this" or "Nothing will stop us."
2. Focus on what you can control.
3. Remind members of the group's important and positive mission.
4. Remind the group how it solved a similar problem before.
5. Focus on problem solving, not blaming.

Solving Problems Proactively

1. Anticipate problems and address them before they happen.
2. Take the initiative to understand and get what you need to be effective.
3. Do it yourself if others aren't responding. Rely on yourself, not others.

Building External Relationships

1. Create opportunities for networking and interaction.
2. Ask about the needs of other teams.
3. Provide support for other teams.
4. Invite others to team meetings if they might have a stake in what you are doing.

It is not about harmony, lack of tension, and all members liking each other; it is about acknowledging when harmony is false, tension is unexpressed, and treating others with respect. The following table outlines some of the small things that groups can do to establish the norms that build group emotional intelligence.

Originally published in March 2001
Reprint R0103E

About the Contributors

JOSEPH L. BOWER is the Donald K. David Professor
of Business Administration at Harvard Business School
in Boston.

CLAYTON M. CHRISTENSEN is the Robert and Jane Cizik
Professor of Business Administration at Harvard Business
School in Boston.

VANESSA URCH DRUSKAT is an associate professor of
organizational behavior and management at the Whittemore
School of Business at the University of New Hampshire.

RANJAY GULATI is a professor at Harvard Business School
in Boston.

LYNDA GRATTON is a professor of management practice at
London Business School and a senior fellow at the Advanced
Institute of Management.

TAMARA J. ERICKSON is a principal researcher and Executive
Vice President of nGenera, a firm serving senior executives with
leading-edge intellectual capital and action-oriented business
solutions.

PHILIP EVANS is a senior vice president in the Boston office
of the Boston Consulting Group.

MORTEN T. HANSEN is Professor in Entrepreneurship and Area Coordinator of the Entrepreneurship and Family Enterprise Department at INSEAD.

JONATHAN HUGHES is a partner at Vantage partners, a Boston-based consulting firm focused on strategic relationship management.

MATT MARX is a doctoral student at Harvard Business School in Boston.

BOLKO VON OETINGER is a senior vice president in the Munich office of the Boston Consulting Group and is the director of the firm's Strategy Institute.

MICHAEL E. RAYNOR is a director of the Toronto office of Deloitte Consulting.

HOWARD H. STEVENSON is the Sarofim-Rock Professor of Business Administration at Harvard Business School in Boston. He is also chairman of the board for Harvard Business School Publishing.

JEFF WEISS is a partner at Vantage partners, a Boston-based consulting firm focused on strategic relationship management.

BOB WOLF is a manager in the Boston office of the Boston Consulting Group.

STEVEN B. WOLFF is a research consultant at HayGroup where he conducts research and analysis related to various aspects of leadership and organizational effectiveness including emotional intelligence, organizational climate, and leadership.

Index